MOVING STILL

MOVING

STILL

Uncovering the True Stories Behind
Sixteen Forgotten Photographs

Columbia University
Graduate School of Journalism
New York, NY

https://journalism.columbia.edu

ISBN 978-0-578-67804-7

CONTENTS

FOREWORD

Who are they?

Who is the young woman looking at the camera? What's distracting the woman on her left? Who is the man in the baseball uniform? Why are his hands in the air? The women at the long counter — where are they? Is it lunchtime someplace?

Who is that man? Why is he screaming? Who is the young man in the silly hat? Where is he, and what are all those people doing behind him? What about the young man with the shaved head and the face tattoo? Or the woman with the fetching smile? Or the man in the suit and tie with the forbidding look. The baby. The man on the bicycle.

Who are they?

At some point, someone with a camera captured a moment in each of their lives. The moment is at once frozen, and alive. Alive, because what happened in those moments raises questions. And those questions set journeys in motion.

These are the stories of 16 photographs. Many of the people in these photographs are familiar to the writers who have chosen to tell the stories behind them. Some died long before the writers could ever meet them. Others are complete strangers.

If you look at the photos long enough, they begin to come to life. They are moving, even as they are still.

Michael Shapiro

Marina, at Twenty

SCHOOL was a bore. University was short-lived but worse. The future was not worth worrying about. It was already lunchtime by the time Marina woke up. She'd been waitressing at Rox past three in the morning, making it through her shift by constantly topping up a half-pint glass of Stella Artois which had now caught up with her. She looked out of the window and took gulps from a big bottle of Tab.

The city had been awake for hours. Outside her window, Glasgow was gloomy and imposing, its colors gray, black, brown, sandstone mingling with dark soot. It was a smoky, damaged, beautiful place.

Until a few years earlier, Glasgow had been intimidating. Industry was failing. Garbage strikes left piles of rotting trash to flood the streets. Electrical worker walkouts saw lengthy blackouts and no heat even as it froze outside. Gangs fought with violent gusto. The starved economy left the city's buildings in disrepair. Glasgow heaved and sighed in exhaustion.

Marina had grown up in that Glasgow. She could not wait to leave. Her family had been among the lucky ones; they had gas heating so the blackouts weren't as painful for them and her Italian mother always knew how to keep five kids fed. Marina had gone to Catholic school where she hated the nuns — she thought them "strictly non-visionary" — and she was pretty sure they hated her back. Glasgow was a city of religious bigotry and partisanship. Protestants hated Catholics and vice versa. After school Marina was bullied by the posher Protestant schools, a target because of the dated brown velour hat, which was part of her uniform, and her violin. For "fun" — Marina didn't think it was fun — she and her siblings went to the Victorian baths. The highlight of the trip was a watery hot chocolate and a packet of Golden Wonder smokey bacon crisps to be enjoyed on the rainy walk home.

She left Glasgow as soon as she could, aged 17, for university in Edinburgh, where she immediately fell in with a very dodgy crowd of drug-takers and amateur hookers, one of whom later died of a heroin overdose. Her university career involved very little studying or working — she could have papered her walls with the increasingly angry letters she received from lecturers and tutors — and ended after two years when Marina was kicked out of school. She found herself back in Glasgow, in her 20s, permanently broke, subsisting on popcorn and ketchup, but with a wealth of time and freedom.

She had returned a different person, only to find a very different Glasgow.

To be young and broke in Glasgow in the 1980s was to live a fragile existence that had an odd, double-pronged effect. On the one hand, it made you very aware of the insecurity of your life. On the other, it made you reckless. Nothing was forever. You could change or flounce out of jobs because there'd always be another one. Shitty work, but easy to get. Nobody ever asked for qualifications. Needless to say, Marina did not move back in with mom and dad.

Instead, she found a place to live on the West End and discovered the city that had once been home to her unhappy, childhood self, was now teeming with hectic, exciting life.

Especially if you were young.

∞

Glasgow was divided by geography, by style and by class. The West End that Marina had known growing up was filled with grand architecture, art museums and botanical gardens. The poorer and more industrial East End was dominated by crime, tower blocks and huge housing estates known as "schemes." To be called "schemey" was a real Glasgow insult. As a child, Marina was not forbidden to go to the East End — not that she would have listened anyway — but she didn't go out of her way to journey across town. The gangs fought on the East End. It was thought of as dangerous and best avoided, which is what most people living in the West End bubble did.

What little interaction Marina did have with the East End was limited to her stall at the Barras, the indoor market. She sold what she remembers as "a load of old shite," but then so did everyone else. Venturing across the market for a cup of tea and some carrot cake, she often came back to find all her wares stolen. The building was old and crumbling, the floor made of creaky wooden boards above wet mud. One day Marina discovered she had a flea infestation from the water rats that lived underneath the boards. That was the end of the stall.

But some nights out would find Marina in the East End. In edgy pubs like Saracen's Head — known as "*Sarry Heid*" — where they served a drink called the White Tornado, which got you very drunk very fast. Regulars called it "electric soup." When she opened her mouth to speak at the bar, locals, hearing her West End accent, often asked, "*Which part of England do ya come fae?*" These East End adventures were regarded as dangerous madness by her less intrepid friends.

Not that this discouraged her from going back.

∞

Like the city itself, young Glasgow was divided by tribes: the Punks, the Shoegazers, the Art Schoolers, the New Romantics. There were also the Neds, whom Marina avoided. The Neds were the angry young men who were not quite gang members but exuded a certain violent edge. They hung out in the center of town. Marina remembers a chant from one Ned subtribe which wore bizarre, many-buttoned trousers from a tailor called Arthur Black. It went, "Arthur Blacks and tartan braces / We're the boys who'll rip your faces." It was best to stay away. The Shoegazers were gloomy indies who wore anoraks — normcore before normcore was invented. The New Romantics were typically fans of the likes of Spandau Ballet and Duran Duran, which Marina regarded as beneath contempt (although she did love Adam and the Ants). The Art Schoolers, though, she was envious of them, the creative force behind the city's vibrant art and music scene. She wished she had gone to art school, too.

Then there were the rich kids, the living incarnation of conspicuous consumption, driving around in fancy cars and hoofing cocaine.

Marina felt most kinship with the Punks, though her style was more glam rock.

∞

Marina waited tables at Rox, a restaurant in the center of town. It served pretty much everything and, while not posh, it was cool. Rox was in the basement of a music bar called Rock Garden. Last orders were at 2 a.m. and she and the other staff always stayed on for drinks after. They would drink lager because it was the easiest to steal undetected. They'd cook up steaks from the kitchen and somehow never got caught.

The guy who owned Rox — who later had to flee the country after drug charges were brought against him — would go to New York City as often as he could and steal all the good ideas. He made the staff wear mint green boiler suits. Menus were on plexiglass clipboards. Furniture was white and curvilinear. The place was always mobbed. Marina worked a nine-hour shift and always went home exhausted.

∞

When she wasn't witnessing Rox's extremely short chef mount an overturned pot in order to grope one of the waitresses, Marina found working at Rox to be quite fun. Everyone would come in: bands, actors, designers. The singer Harry Nilssen came in with the bosses of Radio Clyde. He loved Marina so much he left her a £20 tip — a ridiculously generous amount in those days — and, the following morning, the boss of Radio Clyde got his personal assistant to phone and offer her a job. She said no.

She finally quit when the manager, known for being an unstable drunk, pinned her up against the wall, leaving bruise marks down her arms. He was mad at her for not being able to carry two soups at the same time. Marina's father told her she must have done something to deserve it.

∞

Marina and her flatmate, Christine, lived in the middle floor drawing room of what used to be a big house, split into apartments. They had a huge window that overlooked the gardens. The kitchen was a tiny, windowless cupboard. But then they seldom cooked and when they did, they rarely did the dishes — they'd toss them out rather than clean them. They had a clam-shell shaped vinyl sofa with a big stain left from spilled black currant juice that no one had ever bothered to wipe up.

Christine would wake up hours after Marina. She worked at Rox too and was, like all of them at the time, an absolute pisshead. She and Marina were best friends. Christine liked to talk about when she dated Bryan Ferry, just one of her many claims to fame. If Marina and Christine didn't fancy leaving the house, they would watch the Muppets on TV. And if that wasn't on they'd watch snooker — mostly when they were stoned because they liked the colors. In their more cutting-edge moments, they would tape the songs they liked off "Top of the Pops," so they'd have music ready to play when they had friends around, on video, an exciting social innovation.

∞

One night, Marina was getting ready to go out. Her hair was styled with Pluko pomade into a bleach blonde helmet. She applied thick, dark eyebrow pencil and an equally thick coat of lipstick. Next came the false eyelashes and nails. Her outfit was an old man's suit, found in a vintage store, a good three sizes too big. She cinched the trousers in at the waist with a silk orange tie and put on an enormous pair of platform shoes. Her friend Derek called on the landline and they arranged to meet with Marina's boyfriend, David, outside Maestro's, a club near the art school.

Marina always liked to dress differently and in Glasgow, this meant you were the subject of much mockery. A passerby, seeing her dressed in a brown corduroy sack dress, matching brown hat and big platform shoes — always platforms — yelled at her, *"Haw hen are you out for your Halloween?"*

Marina's taste was eclectic, threading together different styles from different eras. She loved glam rock: Roxy Music and David Bowie, even T. Rex. Mixed in some psychobilly, just for the sleazy-glamorous, swamp-rockiness of it all. And, of course, Marina's at-home bleach job was designed after Debbie Harry.

Marina was waiting outside the club when she heard the familiar clanking sound of her friends approaching. David and Derek, both enthusiastically tattooed at a time when it was really only gang members who were inked, had arrived, clad in black leather — David's hair hidden under a black leather studded cap and Derek's defying gravity in the form of a very large blue mohawk. They were dripping with chains, on their wrists, around their necks and connecting belts to trousers. The doormen at Maestro's took one look and turned them all away.

So they made their way East and found themselves at Glasgow's own Grand Ole Opry. Until that night, the club had been populated only by Glasgow's country and western fanatics. No one there minded how Marina, David and Derek looked. They drank 40-pence vodka doubles and joined the wee wifies with gray perms in dancing something called the "slosh," a line dance that everyone knew — with their slippers on. They watched the gunslinging competition and the end-of-the-night unfurling of the American flag, while Elvis sang "An American Trilogy." Audience participation was encouraged: Derek and David were invited on stage to tunelessly bellow "Sunset of My Tears." The Opry-goers love it: people cheered *"gaun yersels, boys!"*

∞

One day, Marina woke up with some time to think as she drank her Tab and looked out over Glasgow from her window. The city she loved was starting to feel too small. It had served her well as the vibrant backdrop for her 20s. But, once again, she had grown and the city had changed.

When she looks at this photograph of her friends at a party in the early 1980s, she no longer recognizes their lives, their concerns, their hedonism. Most of the characters have faded from her life. She's still friends with Derek. He stands on the left, next to Annie who is in the middle, looking into the camera. Neither she nor Derek recognizes the woman on the right, whose eyes have turned elsewhere.

The friends would go wherever you could get massively dressed up and where free drinks were abundant. Marina recalls that the party where this photograph was taken was for the launch of a new band at a bar called Nico's, a faux Parisian brasserie. Bands would always hang out at Rox, so to work at Rox would get you on guest lists all over town.

With the coming of a new decade, Marina decided it was time to leave. London was waiting.

Circe Hughes *is a print and video journalist from London, England, who covers politics, climate change and arts and culture. She previously interned at i-D London and her work has been featured in the Brooklyn Ink. Pandemic permitting, Circe aspires to find a job, preferably in video journalism. In her spare time, she likes to lose her keys and find them again.*

Glory

GLORY always believed she was different, that she was destined for big things, that she was going to be a star. Glory knew she would need to leave Chicago.

She grew up on the southside, and as the second oldest of six children, it would fall to her to help care for her younger siblings. She was good at it, so good that when a friend of her mother wanted her to care for her toddler daughter she asked for Glory, who was happy to help. She liked children. The families were close. Glory, meanwhile, was 17 and had a lot to learn if she was going to make her big dreams come true.

The little girl's name was Margo. She was four years old and Glory took her everywhere. Many mornings, Glory would walk down South Cottage Grove to the Abraham Lincoln Center for lessons in dance and theater. She carried a duffel bag over one shoulder and carried Margo on her hip. She took her to Edna Somerville Oates' ballet and modern dance class almost every day. As she practiced her dancing in the front room Margo toddled in the back. It was understood, wherever Glory was, Margo was there too.

"She was like my little baby," Glory would later say. "Everywhere that I went, that kid was right there with me."

On Saturday afternoons they went to the movies. They hopped the bus and headed down to 39th Street. Glory would recall how Margo, giggling and excited, could barely contain herself the whole way down. They would get popcorn to share. More often than not, Margo would fall asleep in her lap while Glory watched the movie. Afterward, the two would sit at the soda counter of the drug store and order milkshakes.

"They were like mother and daughter," says Glory's eldest sister, Lynn Colton.

Margo's mother, Mary Smith, was a beauty. "The kind of woman who would stop traffic," says Glory. "She was a socialite and she loved parties. My mother was the same way, a lot of women were at the time." As she continues, it becomes clear that their mothers, though available to their children, were more concerned with things other than parenting.

Margo's father, Harold Smith or "Smitty," worked as a waiter aboard the

Pennsylvania Railroad line. Each week, he would travel out of Chicago, serving passengers all the way across the country and back. He would say that with all the time and steps spent on that job, he'd walked the equivalent of Chicago to Florida. It was a good and steady job at a time when such jobs were scarce for Black men. But, Smitty was preferred to work the railroad because he was a fair-skinned man. He was White "passing." And though all those around him knew he really was a bi-racial, Black man, it was to his benefit to be ambiguous to those who wouldn't know the difference.

He worked long days and weeks and spent a lot of the time away. While his wife Mary was with their infant son Pedro, Glory looked after Margo.

Glory was tall and mature beyond her years. She got a job at a five and dime because people thought she was older than she was.

Glory spent many nights at the library, inside the same Abraham Lincoln Center where she was training in dance and theater by day. Even there Margo was by her side. At the end of the evening, Glory would take Margo home and put her to bed, some nights with her mother still in the next room. She would wait for Margo to fall asleep before sneaking out to head home roughly eight to ten blocks away.

"She would start shrieking and crying like a little bird, calling out to me Gurio, Gurio!" recalls Glory. "And she'd run out on the balcony and look down to see if she saw me coming out of the door and going down Oakwood Boulevard. She would call back to me, breaking my little heart. And all that crying would make her mother crazy. I had to come back because I didn't want her screaming like that. When she was so upset, all I wanted to do was calm her down."

"I would bring her back home with me many nights. My siblings would tease, 'Here she goes with that Margo again.' But truly she was welcome and loved by my family. It was one more mouth to feed. One more head in the bed. But she was our family, for many years."

∞

In 1953, Glory was backstage for what would be one of her last performances at the Abraham Lincoln Center. As the curtains closed, Glory turned to the wings to exit. Waiting on the side to speak with her was Gloria Houseman, an actress who had been featured in Richard Wright's "Native Son."

Houseman knew that the young Glory was set to attend the Encampment for Citizenship summer program in New York City. And knowing that she had a path to get to New York, she pulled Glory aside, looked her in the eyes and said, "Glory, when you go to New York, you must not come back to Chicago. There is nothing here for you."

But for Glory, this message was a culmination of all the things that she already believed about herself, that she was destined for great things. She had known it since she was five. She was going to make it big on Broadway. She would be like the performer she modeled herself after, Mary Martin, who could sing, dance and act.

So, she devised a plan kept secret that she shared only with her sister and grandmother. She packed not for the summer, but for a one-way trip: "I would stay in New York, go into theater and do the things I needed to do."

And that meant leaving Margo. She was too young to realize that this departure wasn't just for the summer or for a few weeks like before. This was a true separation. More than just blocks between them, but hundreds of miles apart.

There would be no more dance classes. No more movie and ice cream outings, and no more "Gurio" coming to comfort her in the middle of the night.

A year later, Margo's mother gave birth to Margo's youngest brother, only to die a few days later. Her father, who had been away for work, returned to Chicago as the widowed father of four children. Margo, now nine, immediately called Glory.

"When Margo called me, she was hysterical. All she could say was, 'Please come get me, please come get me,'" Glory recalls. "It broke my heart that I couldn't be with her, but there was nothing I could do." Glory was now just 19 and knew she couldn't care for Margo and her siblings in the way that they needed.

Having finished her summer program, Glory was now auditioning and training. She had moved to an all-girls dormitory at the International YMCA in West Village and found a job as a shorthand secretary to a speechwriter for the American Jewish Committee.

An early recommendation from actress Cicely Tyson to audition with director Vinette Carroll propelled Glory into the world which she felt she belonged.

Parts began coming her way. "Things came to me," she says, "and I was ready for them."

She had made her sister, Lynn, promise to look after Margo and her siblings, who with their father so often away were living with his mother. When their late mother's family attempted to step in and split them up in order to "ease the pressure" of one family having to potentially take in four children, Lynn refused to let them.

"I guess I was the wild one because I packed a 38-snub nose," said Lynn. "When they came and tried to take those kids away, I met them at the door with it cocked and, in my hand. They didn't have no problems, because they were attached to us."

Still, Lynn and Glory knew that the children needed a mother. When the time came for Smitty to find a new wife, it was Lynn who sat him down and demanded he list the names of every single woman in town that he knew. Two years later he remarried.

∞

Glory Vance Scott would go on to perform as a principal dancer with Katherine Dunham, Talley Beatty and other dance companies including the American Ballet Company. She performed on Broadway in "House of Flowers," "Kwamina," "The Great White Hope," and in the 1974 motion picture "The Wiz." She later earned a Ph.D., became a published author and founded Dr. Glory's Youth Leadership Theater.

"My whole world was full and rich," says Glory. "And I have no regrets." She is now 87 and lives in New York.

Margo grew to have an abundant life. Now the vice president of development at a hospital not far from where she and Glory first met, she's dedicated over 40 years of her life's work to serving Chicago as a hospital administrator and philanthropist.

Through the years, Margo married and had two children and six grandchildren, one of whom is me.

As for Glory, Margo says, "She'd find time to write and send me pictures all the time. She has beautiful penmanship and she'd always write with a black fountain pen. You always knew you were getting something good in the mail from her."

"We would hear from her every two to three months. You know, just to write and to let us know that, 'You know, I may be doing well, but I haven't forgotten about you. I miss you and I love you.' You know, that's the kind of person she is. Even to this day."

Hayley Vaughn *is a multimedia, print and broadcast journalist from Chicago, Ill. She covers general news, race and culture, women's issues, food and politics. She previously worked in PR and communications at ESSENCE Magazine and at Time, Inc. in brand communications for InStyle, ESSENCE, Travel & Leisure and People en Espanol. Hayley hopes to work as a producer at a major news network after graduation. When she's not reporting, she doubles as an avid home chef and foodie. She always makes time for brunch, good books and dancing with friends.*

The Big Life

THERE was a photograph of my great-grandmother on the cover of Sports Illustrated that sat on the wooden countertop in an old-fashioned barroom of a stately southern mansion in rural Georgia. The house, where my grandparents spent the winter hunting and fishing, had been passed down to my grandmother by her mother, whom we knew as Granny. I'd look at the photo during my family's annual Christmastime visit. Every time I entered the bar area to refill a bowl of popcorn or pistachios, it sat there, propped up in a solitary frame surrounded by cocktail glasses.

It reminded me of a scene one might see on "Downton Abbey," like a fancy couple out for a shoot in the English countryside.

Granny appeared on the cover of the magazine in 1958. She was one of the first women to do so, and certainly one of the first women to wear something other than a bathing suit. She stands in the background of the photograph, out of focus. She's clutching a 20-gauge shotgun at her chest with both hands. Her second husband, my step-great-grandfather, stands crisply in the foreground. He holds his shotgun at the ready. His gaze is firm. Granny meanwhile is in motion, but aimlessly so. The barrel of her gun faces toward the sky as if she has no intention of shooting anything.

Her being on the cover had nothing to do with her own accomplishments other than having married the man to her left.

But this was not a source of disappointment for Granny, as I was to learn. Quite the opposite. She once told one of her granddaughters that she should aspire to "the big life." She did not believe the big life was possible for women who, say, married their high school sweethearts and stayed in places like St. Louis, where she grew up.

∞

In some ways, my great-grandmother's life started big from the outset. She was born in St. Louis in 1904. Her father was a highly regarded surgeon who figured regularly on the pages of local newspapers. The newspapers reported when he fixed a broken arm and spoke at banquets, and one paper dedicated a whole paragraph to say that he would be away for the weekend on a visit to Kentucky. When Granny was 19 months old, the St. Louis Globe-Democrat reported that she had swallowed some sort of decorative brooch pin at 8:30 a.m. Luckily, the pin was removed and she made a quick recovery.

Granny was off to a good start by way of her father's renown. But as a woman, she would have to marry well to maintain her status.

She grew up to be a remarkably beautiful woman — a real *femme fatale*, according to those who knew her. Her siblings called her "Mizz Exquiz," a reference to her exquisite looks. As an adolescent, Granny was pursued by men such as Black Jack Bouvier, the father of Jackie Kennedy. She was only 20 when she married her first match, who was called Babe. They had a daughter — my grandmother — shortly thereafter.

Like Granny, Babe was known around St. Louis for his good looks. He was the life of the party. He often carried around his guitar and ukulele for spontaneous one-man shows.

Granny, Babe and their daughter moved into a garage apartment in downtown St. Louis. It belonged to Babe's parents. Depending on who you talk to, their living arrangement was either impoverished or perfectly comfortable. But if her story is a "rags to riches" tale, then that point in her life was certainly the "rags" portion of it.

By most accounts, Babe became a chronic alcoholic. Whether he was always that way or developed a problem over time is unclear. Everyone has a similar way of describing his condition. He was at turns "a fall-down drunk," a "knock-down drunk," or a "fall-down, knock-down alcoholic." His life didn't seem to be going anywhere, and certainly not toward the life Granny sought. She had to make a change.

Whether it was true love, self-preservation or a mix of both, she found her new investment at a storied dinner party sometime in the late 1930s. Not everyone who knew Granny remembered hearing the story of that night, but those who did said she spoke of it like it was magic.

It took place at a cliffside mansion overlooking the Mississippi River in Alton, Ill. Flanked by Babe, she walked into the grand dining room, which had ceilings at least 20 feet high. It was a room that was built for impressing and entertaining guests. The mansion belonged to the man who would become Granny's second husband. But who he was isn't important — he was Granny's ticket to the big life.

One family member recalls hearing that there was a big storm that night — a typical St. Louis storm with lightning and thunder and the works — that knocked the power out. Perhaps Granny and the host went off somewhere in the darkened house. But that's pure speculation, according to another family member's interjection.

Regardless of what happened that night, it was certainly consequential because two years later, Granny had a new husband. He was a fabulously wealthy, self-made man, 11 years her senior. He would shape the rest of her life and generations to come.

She had found her big life. So began the riches portion of the story.

Granny and her daughter moved into her new husband's mansion. Spectacular setting aside, they were quite isolated there. Alton was a small river town. There were factories on the other side of the river — they made pennies, quarters, copper, guns and ammunition — that also belonged to her husband.

Before long, Granny persuaded her husband to move back to St. Louis, where she could restore her lively social life. They bought a house there and then an apartment in New York City. Then came the vacation homes in East Hampton, Georgia and the Bahamas. As the seasons changed, they moved from one house to the next, spending much of the summer in the Hamptons and much of the winter in rural Georgia, with interspersed trips to the Bahamas.

In the scheme of her life goals, Granny was off to the races. She and her daughter would have all the opportunities imaginable to her. She had beautiful jewelry, clothes and art; extravagant houses with gardens and fabulous company to fill them.

Her new husband adored her. Although she was in some ways a traditional wife, she was also said to be the one who "wore the pants." He fell in love with her not only because she was beautiful, but because she was his opposite. She was outspoken and funny. Meanwhile, "Granddaddy was quiet," one of his granddaughters said.

Maintaining her many houses and entertaining guests took up much of her time. With her husband's money came influence and important people wanted to meet him. Titans of industry and government were not uncommon guests around the dinner table. While her husband was a formidable businessman, Granny was a formidable host. She had a sensational "gift of the gab."

But her day-to-day routine was stagnant: bicycling around the Hamptons, going out to lunches and dressing for dinner.

She did manage to keep life exciting by making things more complicated than they needed to be. Her husband was always dragging her along on fishing trips to a remote part of Canada or their house in the Bahamas. The solitude of those places bored her, as did the fishing. On a windy day in the Bahamas, while her husband was out fishing, Granny decided to have her staff drain the entirety of the pool. At the bottom, she set up a lounge chair so that she could properly sunbathe, now protected from the wind.

As she rotated from one house to the next, she started to tire of her routine and the company she kept. The big-wig types weren't any better companions than her interior designer or her maid. What had previously seemed out of reach became mundane.

"She had a low tolerance for boring people," my uncle said. If you couldn't carry a conversation, Granny had no time for you and didn't care a bit about offending you.

Her husband died in 1982, when he was 89 and Granny was 78. She was left with his money and even less to do. Her world became smaller. Her need for entertainment persisted even as she traded her sun chair for a wheelchair.

She sometimes revealed her dissatisfaction with harsh words for her family members, once announcing to the dinner table after a couple of drinks that she "knew" they only liked her for her money.

In the summers, Granny would invite all of her grandchildren to visit her beach house in East Hampton. Thrust in the entryway to the beach would be Granny in her wheelchair, and a chair by her side. Anyone who wanted to access the beach had to sit in the chair and talk to her for a while. If you wanted to go to the beach, she'd say, you'd have to pay the toll.

What could they offer her? How could they interest her? She wanted to know if they were "big life" people, too.

As age gave way to restlessness, Granny turned to younger family members to fill up her life. She had her favorites. The chosen ones say she was quite fun to go out with. Even in her 80s, when Granny was living alone in her New York City apartment, she was always up to see "what the cats and dogs were doing" out there in the world.

The Sports Illustrated cover captured Granny's attainment of the big life. But a big life can always be bigger, and for Granny, it never felt big enough.

Serena McNiff *is a general-interest journalist from Philadelphia, Pa. She has a particular affinity for science and public health and has written stories on real estate, crime, public transportation and firearms. In the past, she worked for Bold TV, a digital news show, and is currently an intern at HealthDay, a health news site for consumers and medical professionals. When she's not reporting, she's researching the best movies and TV shows, even if she doesn't end up watching them.*

Havasi and her Daughters

MY grandfather never told the story of his grandmother. We never asked because when her name was mentioned he would tear up. We knew about the Armenian Genocide not because it was spoken about at home, but because we learned about it in the Armenian private school my parents sent us to in Encino, Calif.

I knew, vaguely, that some members of my family had escaped the genocide. After living in Syria and then what became Soviet Armenia, those who survived eventually came to the United States in 1976. But I knew nothing of the details of their flight or what set it in motion. That is, until I was in my early 20s and heard for the first time, from my mother, the name Havasi.

In this photograph, Havasi is sitting on the ground holding her granddaughter, Perchui. The photograph was taken around 1939 in Aleppo, Syria. The man in the military uniform was her son-in-law, Sarkis Hovhanessian. On his left stands her daughter, Nvart Hovhanessian. The little man holding a stick-like object was her grandson, Onnik. His brother, Misak, stands to his left holding a shotgun. The rest are unknown.

The fact that they were in Aleppo and that Havasi's daughter was married with three children is remarkable. One and a half million Armenians were starved, tortured, raped and murdered by the Turks in the genocide. Havasi and her family somehow escaped, but like so many of those who did, their freedom came with a price. In this case, the price for a choice Havasi made.

∞

Before the genocide, Havasi and her family lived under the authority of the Ottoman Empire, in a town called Anchrti. She lived with her two daughters, Nvart and Arousiag. Her son had died years earlier from whooping cough when he was five years old. Her husband, Boghos, moved to America and lived in Boston, Mass. Boghos, Havasi and her daughters had initially planned to immigrate to America together. But Havasi had glaucoma and was denied entry before they could set sail. The family was far from rich, so Havasi had to work as a housekeeper.

Word of the killings began as rumors. Armenian officials who worked in the Ottoman government advised people to seek refuge, to hide and prepare for what was to come.

Massacres of the Armenians date back to the 1890s, so my family believes the genocide came to Anchrti at the end of March 1915, weeks before the official start date on April 24. The chief of police in their town ordered Havasi and her daughters, and every other Armenian, to gather at the river for an important announcement concerning their people. She, and so many other Armenians, did as they were told. Havasi and her daughters joined in a march to the river. Arousiag, the older daughter, began walking ahead. Havasi and Nvart followed.

Havasi had worked for many Turkish families and as she walked, a Turkish man recognized her. The man approached Havasi and pulled her and Nvart inside his home.

"Don't go," he told them. "The soldiers are going to kill you."

Havasi was frantic. "My older daughter is ahead," she told the Turkish man, "I have to get her."

They tried to run to get Arousiag, but the Turkish man blocked their way.

"No," said the man. "If you go, you will all be killed."

The Turkish man led them to the back of his home and told them to hide under a pile of hay. They soon heard cries and screams from a distance.

Havasi and Nvart hid in dirt and grime for several hours. When the soldiers came back to check the houses of the Turks to see if anyone was hiding an Armenian, Havasi and Nvart held their breath. Nvart would remember how she and her mother buried themselves under the hay, making sure they covered their mouths so their weeping for her lost sister could not be heard. "The cries," she later said, "got lost in the hay."

They were in survival mode, so Havasi and Nvart began working for the Turkish family again. The Turkish man grew fond of Nvart and encouraged the idea of a union between her and his son. Havasi and Nvart were hesitant. But they were poor, and he had saved their lives. So, instead of refusing the proposal, they devised a plan to flee.

Nvart told the father that her own father lived in Syria and that she and her mother were going to visit him. The Turkish father agreed and allowed them to leave, not knowing they would never come back.

∞

My family does not know the details of their escape to Syria. By 1924, Nvart, who was now in her early 20s, married a man named Sarkis Selveryan. Sarkis had his own story after the genocide. Back in his hometown of Arabgir, he had gone on a killing spree targeting Turkish officials while intoxicated. The Turks put a ransom on his head. A Catholic priest offered to help him escape to Syria in return for his conversion to Catholicism. But the Turks still pursued him. When news reached Aleppo that the Turks were looking for him, one of Havasi's relatives, trying to hide Sarkis's identity, arranged to have his name changed to Hovhanessian.

∞

Nvart and Sarkis had three children, but the marriage was not a happy one. Sarkis began to drink and Nvart would often tell him, "I should have married the Turk instead of you." Still, they planned to leave Syria and return home to Armenia. Besides, Sarkis had a new, common name, and they hoped the Turks would not find him.

A relative of Havasi's intervened and, with the help of her relative's friends, the family boarded a ship in 1946. Havasi, Nvart and her husband, with their children, were included in the first round of families to return back to Armenia — now under Soviet rule. People on board checked in with volunteers who had lists indicating the cities, or towns, the families were assigned to live in. Misak, who was 21 years old, was a volunteer in charge of the list for Armenians. Our family was assigned to live in Stepanavan, a town 85.5 miles away from the capital city of Yerevan. Misak was unhappy with the assigned location and complained to the ship's captain.

"Well, Misak," the captain said, "the paper is in your hands and so is the pen." He caught on and changed our family's location to Yerevan.

My family arrived in Armenia and found refuge in the basement of a school called Stepan Shahumyan. The basement was tiny, and they were a family of six. Some slept on blankets on the cement floor, and that was how Nvart and Sarkis' son, Onnik, developed pneumonia at 14 years old. We do not know the details, but Havasi sent a message to her husband, Boghos, in America that they were struggling again. He decided to send money by hiding gold coins as clothing buttons. He removed the actual buttons from the garment and placed the gold coin on top of the button. He then covered the button and coin with a cloth and sewed it back onto the clothing to ensure the coin would not be stolen.

Money remained tight. But in 1947, the family moved out of the school basement. They had received a loan from the government, so Havasi joined the rest of her family and built a home on Arabkir Street. After Onnik returned from serving in the Soviet army, he helped finish the job. For the first time in a while, the Mazloumian and Hovhanessian family slept on beds.

My great-great-grandmother Havasi had died from an ear infection around the 1950s. In 1959, Onnik met my grandmother Meri and they had three children; one of whom, my mother, was named after her grandmother Nvart. It was no surprise that Sarkis died of alcoholism many years later. My mother was seven years old when she found her grandfather lifeless on the couch.

∞

The last time my family fled their homeland was in 1976. My mother was 12 years old when she watched her father assemble massive wooden containers in the basement of their home. The purpose was to store the family's belongings to be shipped off to America from Soviet Armenia.

They decided to leave their homeland forever. It would take six months for the shipment to reach Los Angeles by boat — so they had to move quickly. Onnik was a woodworker contracted by the government to make high-end furniture. However, he also worked in secret. But every neighborhood had a spy — someone who would report to government officials of illegal activity, and that was how my grandfather got caught. The police kept an eye on Onnik, and after one of the check-ins, he knew he had to hurry to finish so the family could leave Armenia for good.

They arrived in Los Angeles and after they settled in, it hit him.

"For the first time in my life," said Onnik, "I don't hear my heartbeat." My mother never forgot the moment her father opened up to her. After that, he rarely did.

"So what happened to your family after the genocide?" she once asked him. But he only explained how they fled. So when my mother asked him to describe the events, he said, "It's too painful to talk about," which suggested, perhaps, that even though Onnik had never witnessed the genocide, he had grown up hearing the stories.

Onnik, the little boy in the photo, was our last connection to Havasi, whose decision to leave her eldest daughter behind, had spared her family. But it was Onnik's niece, Perchui's daughter, who had gathered the details of Havasi and Nvart's escape, making sure their trauma was preserved before Nvart's death from heart complications on January 25, 1989.

The Ottomans and their successors had tried to rid the nation of Armenians. That led to the beginning of the genocide and to my family's 61-year flight. Havasi and Nvart's survival came at the expense of sacrificing Arousiag, and the decision haunted them. "All the springs," Nvart said, "turned into winters."

Anaïs Amin *is a journalist from Los Angeles, Calif., who covers arts and culture, criminal justice, immigration and conflict. Before attending Columbia Journalism School, she worked at KPFK Radio 90.7 FM in Studio City, Calif. After graduation, she plans to pursue multimedia reporting with a focus on audio and visual storytelling. When she's not reporting, Anaïs likes to paint and watch documentaries.*

Lucky Man

THE casket sat near the altar under the ceiling of St. Gregory the Great Church. The body had been removed from McCabe's Funeral Parlor a day before. It would soon be taken to St. John's Cemetery in Queens for burial. Rev. Eugene Callahan read the Mass, addressing the meager crowd.

Surely, he would have noticed that those who owed the most to the little man in the coffin were conspicuously absent. Babe Ruth had opted not to attend, instead sending flowers. None of his teammates were there, either. Not Lou Gehrig, Herb Pennock or Waite Hoyt. Not Tony Lazzeri or Earle Combs.

It was January 19, 1935, and the season would start in a little over two months without the Yankees' longtime mascot, the man in the coffin, Eddie Bennett. He had been with them for 14 years. Charles McManus, the team secretary, served as pallbearer along with George Perry, the team's public relations man. The team's owner and beer baron, Col. Jacob Ruppert, and Edward Barrow, the business manager, were both ill.

It was Barrow who first spotted news that Bennett had died. A couple of days prior, Margaret L. Scholtz, Bennett's landlord, had found him in his furnished room at 115 West 84th Street. He had been dead for about an hour and he was alone.

Scholtz had last seen Bennett the day before at around 1:30 p.m. and thought he was drunk. An ambulance transported the body from a ground floor room filled with autographed baseballs, bats and photographs of baseball stars. A morgue attendant marked the word "heart" on a slip of paper. An autopsy revealed that Bennett had died of alcoholism.

The Yankees paid for the funeral and burial, sparing Bennett the humiliation of a pauper's grave. Still, it was a humbling ending for a man who had helped the Yankees win seven American League pennants and three World Series championships.

Or so everyone believed.

∞

Eddie Bennett was born in the Flatbush area of Brooklyn, N.Y., in 1904. Early on, an accident left him with a deformed back. Little is known about his family — Bennett, it seems, never talked about it with the sports reporters who chronicled his curious ascent. We know that he attended Saint Paul's parochial school in Williamsburg.

In 1918 the Spanish flu swept across the nation, killing thousands, among them Bennett's parents. A year later he was working as a courier on Wall Street when he was sacked. "I couldn't run fast enough or something," he would later recall.

The day he lost his job, Bennett found himself walking along the Harlem River Speedway to the Polo Grounds. It was then home to the New York Giants and the Yankees, whose own stadium would not open until 1923. He was feeling, he later said, like "the unluckiest egg in the world."

He was 4-foot-5-inches, disabled and out of work. Walking through the Eighth Avenue entrance, Bennett found the Chicago White Sox and the Yankees in a double-header. The Sox were taking a beating.

It must have been a hot day, or the walk must have made Bennett thirsty. After the Yankees won the first game he slipped under the bleachers to get a sip of water. A center fielder in a White Sox uniform approached him with a no-nonsense look on his face. He was Oscar "Happy" Felsch, a Milwaukeean and one of the dominant hitters in the American League.

"Kid, are you lucky?" he asked Bennett. Hunchbacks were said to be talismans and rubbing their back could bring good luck. And Felsch did just that.

"Well, of course," Bennett replied. Apparently satisfied with the answer, Felsch told his team he'd found a "jinx chaser." Bennett was dragged to the dressing room and then asked to sit on the bench. All he had to do was be lucky and deformed.

In the second game, Felsch tripled and then scored the team's first run. The two teams were tied going into the seventh inning, and the Yankees went ahead in the ninth. But Shoeless Joe Jackson's thunderous homer gave the game to the Sox. Or was it their new mascot?

∞

A baseball team is like a dysfunctional family. The parents are the coaches and the managers. They're mercurial, caring, blow hot and cold but ultimately know what's best for the players, who can often act like children, brilliant and capricious. They want their shoes polished with clear or colored polish. They want someone to run their errands on the road. Luckily there's someone whose job it is to accommodate their every whim. That person is the batboy. One devotion by the Federation of Christian Athletes compared the batboy to Jesus washing the feet of the disciples. "If you have a batboy, thank him today, play catch with him, spend a little time getting to know him."

Baseball players are also very superstitious. Don't step on foul lines. Don't wash your shirt on a winning streak. Always eat chicken before every game. In the 1950s, a professor at North Texas State University and a team of field researchers collected more than 408 superstitions from Denton, Texas. Number 68 was, "If a hunchback appears, touch the hump for good luck." This disconcerting bit of wisdom might well have traveled 1,035 miles from Denton to Happy Felsch's German working-class neighborhood on the north side of Milwaukee. The hand Felsch had extended toward Bennett at the Polo Grounds had, unbeknownst to him, gone further than the boy's back. It had reached deep into the irrational, grasping for something to hold on to.

Bennett wouldn't be the first one to be anointed as a good luck charm. Illustrious bearers of good fortune included Louis Van Zelst, a Philadelphia boy who had a short but successful career as a batboy with the Philadelphia Athletics. He got his twisted back when he fell off a wagon, collapsing his lung. The lung recovered but not Van Zelst's back. In 1909, when he was 14 or 15, Van Zelst went to a baseball game between the Athletics and the Detroit Tigers and was spotted by an A's player. Would he tend the bats for the day? Van Zelst said yes and the Athletics won. Rubbing the mascot's back would bring many more victories to the team. One baseball historian wrote that the boy grew to become a member of the family. He was invited to the wedding of the great Eddie Collins and appeared at a dinner hosted by the Baseball Writers Association of America.

There was another lucky mascot on the market at that time. The 1911 World Series game between the Athletics and the Giants pitted Van Zelst against the New Yorkers' mascot, Charles Victor "Victory" Faust. Faust, who was mentally handicapped, had a gift for vaudeville and provided a much welcome counterpoint to John McGraw, the cantankerous manager. At the World Series, Faust led the band to entertain the crowd gathered in Shibe Park, working his magic any way he could. It wasn't enough. The Giants lost. Asked why the Athletics had won, the legendary Christy Mathewson "pointed the finger at Louis Van Zelst, claiming he out-jinxed Faust," according to a baseball historian.

After his chance encounter with Felsch, the Sox invited Bennett to two more games in New York. The Sox won both. "They were convinced I was a lucky charm," Bennett later told a sports writer. Yet, the team refused to take him on the road to the World Series. Was it because they didn't want to win?

It turned out that Felsch and seven of his teammates had conspired with bookies to throw the series against the weaker Cincinnati Reds in exchange for a $100,000 payoff.

The plot was uncovered and the "Black Sox" conspirators were banned for life. Bennett never lost his fondness for the Sox. Still, he said years later, "It was a terrible blow for me."

Luckily, he was in demand. The Brooklyn Robins hired him in 1920. With Bennett on board, the team, led by the congenial Wilbert Robinson, won its fifth pennant.

The Robins, however, must have thought poorly of Bennett — he wasn't voted a share of the pool money. When the team appeared in the World Series, it was without their mascot. The Robins should have known better. It is said that the batboy cursed the team from afar. The Brooklynites lost to the Cleveland Indians. They would have to wait until 1941 to win another pennant, and until 1955 to win the World Series.

By this point, Bennett's reputation as a winner-maker had crossed the East River and whetted the Yankees' appetite. When The Washington Post wrote that year that "another important capture" had been made by the team's management, one "that is expected to go a long way toward clinching the 1921 pennant," the newspaper wasn't referring to Babe Ruth, sold to them by the Red Sox. It was talking about "Eddie Bennett, who bats way over the .300 mark as a mascot."

On January 28, 1921, Bennett presented himself at the American League office to receive his new uniform. He had just inked a deal with Miller Huggins, the team's manager, and Edward Barrow. He would be paid $25 a week to serve as batboy. The agreement stipulated that should he bring the team a pennant he would also work the World Series.

The season was yet to start, but the Yankees had good reasons to believe in their lucky star. Babe Ruth had hit 54 home runs in 1920, an unheard-of number. And they had their new batboy. "If superstitions are winners, then baseball fans can place their bets on the New York Yankees as the winners of this year's American League race," a journalist wrote at the time. "The big bet is none other than little Eddie Bennett, a cripple."

It was a reductive analysis. The Yankees were shaping up to enter the Roaring Twenties with a blast. The Yankees also picked up pitcher Waite Hoyt from the Red Sox, who would fulfill his promise in New York.

Bennett was the latest addition to the payroll that year. He joined a string of new colorful characters, including a three-year-old named Little Ray Kelly, Babe Ruth's personal mascot.

One picture taken in 1921 shows Bennett proudly wearing his new uniform. His arms are folded over a bomber jacket with the words "New York" emblazoned across the chest. He's wearing a baseball cap adorned with the team's logo. Two strands of hair spill out from under the cap, wet-looking, as if coated in sweat.

"Both are doing much to bring the Yankees home first in the pennant race," a journalist wrote of Ruth and Bennett. "Eddie admits that Babe and the other players are doing great work, but insists that he should not be overlooked when the credit is handed out."

There could not be an odder couple than Bennett and Ruth. Bennett was now 17 and worked alongside the most popular player in baseball. At least two group pictures were taken of the team that year. On each of them, Bennett sits in the front row, like a toy. He takes up so little space that his elbows don't even touch those of the players he's framed by.

What Bennett lacked in frame he made up for in enthusiasm and prudence. He had decided, as one sports commentator put it, that "one of the most important assets of a good caddy was a still tongue."

He was loyal to his team, even in defeat. When it lost an exhibition game he shrugged it away. "Oh Hell," he told a columnist at the Louisville Courier-Journal. "What's a little game like this to us fellows? We didn't try! We don't want to take no chances of getting a leg broke or a sprained wrist."

September saw the New Yorkers win their second pennant in franchise history. Miller Huggins and Edward Barrow made good on their promise: Bennett was on the field when the Yankees faced off against the Giants in the World Series.

On October 6, 1921 readers of the New York Tribune were treated to a collage of "outstanding figures" on the first day of the World Series. Babe Ruth figured prominently. At the bottom of the page was Eddie Bennett, jumping in the air, his arms held high over his head.

∞

In 1922 Bennett was now truly part of the game. He was known both as the Yankees' batboy and mascot and for his services received a $300 share of the World Series money — the Yankees had lost to the Giants in the Series that year — as well as another $200 from Edward Barrow, together roughly $7,700 today.

The New York Tribune ran another photo of him jumping in the air. He bought his first suit. The Yankees treated their mascot well and Bennett knew it. There had been rumors that he might leave New York to join the Washington Senators, but they never materialized.

A year later, the Yankees won their third straight pennant and their first World Series against the Giants at the newly built Yankee Stadium. Every club member got a watch and a gold baseball fob, mascot included.

By the end of 1923, Bennett had amassed enough experience that he thought of writing his memoir, "My Five Years with League Leading Teams." The project, it seems, never came to fruition. The Yankees won their fifth pennant and second World Series in 1927. Each club member got a diamond ring to celebrate the crushing victory against the Pittsburgh Pirates at the World Series. Bennett showed his ring to a newspaperman. "Ain't that swell?" he said proudly.

By this point, it had become apparent to sports commentators that Bennett brought much more than luck to the team. He was, the journalist Westbrook Pegler wrote, a "workman." Traveling with the team during the season, he was at least once in charge of the logistics of transportation and handling baggage, a task usually reserved for the traveling secretary.

He had "developed a sinecure, ordinarily given to the sons of players or stockholders, into a job," Pegler wrote. Bennett had become a lifeline to some of the players. On the road, Urban Shocker, a pitcher afflicted with congenital heart disease, roomed with him. Shocker was worried his teammates might discover his secret, and his career would be over. But he knew he could trust Bennett's "still tongue." His secret came to light only after he died from heart disease and pneumonia in September 1928.

The Yankees won their sixth pennant that year. Bennett was voted a share pool again. He now wore bright ties and well-tailored clothes, when not in a uniform. In December, The Brooklyn Citizen devoted two columns to the rise of Bennett. He was, a journalist wrote, "one of the most envied members of America's younger generation."

In less than ten years, he had established himself as a familiar face on a crowded stage. An orphan, he had found a family in the most successful sports franchise of the Roaring Twenties.

But his luck was running out.

∞

Eddie Bennett had good reasons to be in high spirits at the beginning of 1932. He was contributing his fair share to the Yankees' victories. Or rather, he and his team were. Bringing good luck to the players had become a well-oiled operation. By now he was hiring kids to carry the players' bats for him. This way he could focus on the rituals on the field. He was the first to shake hands with a Yankee after they crossed the plate. Pitcher Wilcy Moore would toss him his first ball at the beginning of warmup. Some players wanted no one to touch their bats but Bennett.

With a new manager, Joe McCarthy, at the helm, the Yankees had high hopes of winning their seventh pennant. As a matter of fact, they blasted through the first 13 games of the season that year, winning ten.

If Bennett was watching over the players, it is unclear whether anyone was doing the same for him. In May, as he crossed the street, a swerving taxicab hit and pinned him against a pillar, breaking one of his legs and sending him to Reconstruction Hospital in Manhattan. For the first time in 11 years, the Yankees were without Bennett.

A photographer with the New York Daily News visited him in the hospital.

He was greeted by Bennett lying in bed, a bandage wrapped around his forehead, one leg in a sling. The picture made it to the front page of the newspaper. "Now that the Yanks' latest winning streak has been broken, they'll need their famous mascot, Eddie Bennett, more than ever," the caption read.

Yet, the team found ways to make do without its lucky charm. Ruth, Lou Gehrig, Tony Lazzeri and Bob Meusel led the Yanks to a seventh pennant. They would face off against the Chicago Cubs in the World Series. Bennett had been standing in the dugout in 1923 and 1927, the two times the Yankees had won the championship. How could the team clinch its third victory without its mascot?

Workmen were draping Yankee Stadium in bunting and flags. More than 41,000 spectators would sit the next day on the stadium's double-decked grandstands. But for now, it was largely empty, save for the players in pinstriped uniforms practicing on the field. Then came another member of the team, hobbling on crutches. Eddie Bennett, his leg still in a cast, wanted to wish the players luck. Wilcy Moore, Earle Combs, Lyn Last and Ben Chapman flocked around him, inquiring about his health.

Bennett, after all, would be able to watch the World Series on the field. The "luckiest mascot" was back in business, and so was his team.

∞

The 1932 World Series is remembered for Babe Ruth's "called shot" and Lou Gerigh's prowess at the bat, not for the man on crutches watching from the sideline. He was now 28 and still performing what many considered a boy's job. Still, he was Eddie Bennett, "the dean of the old pros," as one sportswriter described him. And he watched as the Yankees swept the Series.

Did the best team in baseball history really need a mascot, one who was there only because of a centuries-old superstition? Many years later, the financier Warren Buffet would say it did. "My managerial model is Eddie Bennett," Buffett told a group of Berkshire Hathaway shareholders in 2002. "Eddie understood that how he lugged bats was unimportant; what counted instead was hooking up with the cream of those on the playing field."

Throughout his career, Bennett had repeatedly insisted he had no superstitions. That the secret to the Yankees' grandeur was not on the bench or the bats but "in the players."

But that was before his car accident. On May 24, 1933, Bennett, still on crutches, came into the Yankees' dressing room in Yankee Stadium. He told the players he was there to "chase the jinx." The team won against the Cleveland Indians that day. But it had also won the day before, unassisted by the mascot. Perhaps Bennett was trying to chase a different kind of jinx. After his death, newspapers noted that he had been drinking to chase the pain away.

Marty Appel, a former Yankees public relations director, said this might not have been just a fleeting vice. Little Ray Kelly, Babe Ruth's personal mascot and a longtime friend of Appel, occasionally roomed with Bennett. Appel said Kelly told him, "Eddie was not only malformed," he was "also a drunk."

∞

If they knew Bennett was bibulous, newspapermen refrained from mentioning it in their obituaries when he died in 1935. "Bennett had sublime faith in his powers," the Associated Press wrote the day after his death.

Jimmy Mars, a bellicose youngster, succeeded him as the last of the Yankees' traveling mascots. When he had heard about the accident that left Bennett incapacitated, Mars, sensing his opportunity, ran away from home in Chicago and rode a train to St Petersburg, Fla., where the Yankees were training. He got his lucky break after picking a discarded bat on the practice field and bringing it back to the dugout running. Joe McCarthy noticed him and hired him as a batboy.

Mars had ambition. He hoped that someone would pick up his bat after him one day. But he stopped growing at 5-feet-3-inches, and his dream of one day joining the players on the field was dashed. Unlike Bennett, Mars believed in luck. He carried a copper penny he found on the street. He refused to spend it, even for candy. As years passed, it tarnished in his pocket.

He thought it would bring good luck to the Yankees, who had long believed that their good luck came from Eddie Bennett.

Benoit Morenne *is a journalist from Paris, France, who covers climate change, religion and technology. His work has been featured in The New York Times, The Economist, The Christian Science Monitor, Narratively and Libération. In the future, he hopes to continue to cover climate change and how it intersects with business, religion and technology. In his spare time, Benoit rides his bicycle across New York knowing full well it will get stolen, like every other bicycle he's owned.*

The Long Goodbye

WAVES trailed behind the cargo ship as it sailed out of the Port of Havana. My grandparents and infant mother were on it. So were countless families of political prisoners.

Hundreds had flooded Havana's Malecón to bid farewell. For some, it would be the last time. My grandma's godmother and a friend stood among them as they all waved white handkerchiefs. The only life my grandparents had ever known was coming to an end. Home slipped farther away until Cuba vanished from view.

∞

My grandparents' life together started five years earlier in a small town far from the capital of a very different Cuba.

One day in 1958, my grandma, whom we call Ama, went with her friends and family to a celebration commemorating the anniversary of Santa Lucía's sugar mill. They walked uphill to the town center, which was filled with people, among them a young man who worked for a local brewery, Cristal. The man, who had studied communications, held a megaphone and called out for people to try the beer.

Sometime that afternoon, he met Ama — she does not recall exactly how. They ended up spending the day together once his work was done. They talked and danced. And at the end of the day, he bade her farewell and went home to the nearby city of Holguín.

Ama returned to school in the same city, and over the next two years, they saw each other from time to time. She was studying to be a teacher and believed that a serious boyfriend would be a distraction.

Later, she would say, "I thought, 'Well, if it's meant for me, it will be.'"

The young man would visit her at her grandma's house where they would talk. They went to the movies together and attended Mass. When Ama finished school, she was ready for the young man to become her boyfriend. It was 1960, and Cuba was transforming around them.

∞

Fidel Castro had by then been in power for over a year, having overthrown the dictatorship of Fulgencio Batista on New Year's Eve 1958. Castro's government had enacted its first land reform law limiting landholdings to 993 acres. He had initiated public works projects and nationalization plans. This was to be a new Cuba run for Cubans, by Cubans. "*Cuba Sí*," went the catchphrase of the revolution, "*Yanquis No.*"

The new government was cracking down on political opponents and arresting hundreds of those it deemed counter-revolutionaries. Castro's foes began armed attacks throughout Cuba. In time, they established guerilla bases in the mountains.

Meanwhile, Ama and the young man would climb the steps to the park where they had first met. He recited poetry to her. She liked that.

The government, however, had plans for the young man. They had a use for someone with a truck and a megaphone. He was sent to the city of Varadero to assist with crowd control. But before he left, he had a question for Ama: would she marry him?

She accepted. But the engagement came with one condition: if she married him, she would have to leave Cuba with him.

"I want you to be my wife, but this is Communism," he said. "Things are going to get really ugly here. There isn't going to be food. Things are going to be scarce."

He wasn't the only one who wanted to leave. About 200,000 Cubans fled Cuba for the United States immediately after the revolution. Most of them landed in South Florida and set up their temporary lives. They told themselves Castro would be removed from power soon. They would be able to return home. "*Ojalá*" became their motto. Hopefully.

Ama's father also wanted to leave and told her that getting married was her chance to get out. He promised he would join them as soon as he could — as would her sister and mother.

So Ama agreed. But leaving was not so simple.

∞

The young couple spent most of the year of their engagement apart. They wrote letters to each other while he was away. They spoke on the phone when they could. They saw each other whenever he had the chance to visit. The government requisitioned his truck when they no longer needed him, and he started a new job at a radio station.

Ama and the young man we call Abu were married in Santa Lucía on December 3, 1961. Ama recalls everything about that day as beautiful. A small group joined the newlyweds for the reception that took place in her backyard. There was roast pig with rice and beans, a Cuban tradition. "We didn't have money for anything else," she says with a sigh.

They left for their honeymoon after the reception. They headed to Havana with Abu's cousin and wife, stopping at a roadside motel for the night so that Ama and Abu could have their first night together as husband and wife.

"I got married a virgin, without having been with any other man before," she says, glowing with pride.

They spent their honeymoon with two other couples — the one who had driven them to Havana and my grandma's cousin and her new husband. This was common for them. They often hung out with their families.

The six of them saw the capital. They visited Pinar del Río and Soroa. They spent a night at a popular outdoor spot in Havana that was situated atop a river called Río Cristal. They talked. They drank. They listened to music.

They returned to Holguín a week later. Abu went back to work at the radio station which, like newspapers and broadcast stations across Cuba, was now under government control. Ama was ordered to teach the children whom the regime had separated from their parents and sent to work in the sugar cane fields, commonly referred to as "*El Campo.*"

Ama and her fellow teachers would take a bus from Santa Lucía to the sugar fields and then walk a mile to the schools. Castro's plan was to make all Cubans literate; almost a quarter of them couldn't read. But the teachers were also directed to spread messages of Marxism to children when they were out of their parents' reach.

The fields were controlled by the government too. The teachers were always watched. But, even so, Ama refused to teach her students the new national anthem. When she was questioned, she said she hadn't learned it.

"They did whatever they wanted," she would later say. "They didn't care about the country. They didn't care about anything."

Then, she added, "I lived in a tiny town, and there, we felt everything."

∞

Castro had begun his rule two years earlier with a weeklong "Caravan of Victory" from Eastern Cuba to Havana. He and his 1,000 or so guerilla soldiers were greeted as heroes at every stop on their way to the capital. He delivered his first speech to tens of thousands of admirers the day they arrived in Havana. He talked until dawn and then released a flock of white doves to signify the peace he was going to bring to Cuba. One dove landed on his shoulder — a dark omen; the same thing had happened to Spain's dictator Francisco Franco when he took power.

More and more people left. In 1960, the American government waived immigration restrictions for Cubans. After the first wave of immigration, 14,000 children arrived between then and 1962. The children had been sent to the United States alone to live in foster homes throughout the country until they could be reunited with their parents. It was called *Operación Pedro Pan,* or Operation Peter Pan.

Ama did not recall Batista's reign with fondness. But under Batista, she felt it was possible to live without fear of the government so long as you were not regarded as a threat. That changed under Castro, as Committees for the Defense of the Revolution appeared in every neighborhood. It was not always clear who the informants were.

"In my town, the light went out, and I can't remember if it ever came back," Ama says.

She got pregnant in 1962 and continued teaching. Abu kept working at the station. They went back and forth between Holguín and Santa Lucía. They were biding their time. Their daughter was born in January 1963. The time to leave was fast approaching, though they did not know it.

∞

Abu's father was a man with many connections. He had told Ama and Abu years before that they would be leaving soon, but he shared no details. Time passed with no further word on a plan to leave. "Any day now, our time will come," Ama remembers telling herself.

After the failed Bay of Pigs invasion, Castro agreed to send some of the families of the political prisoners he had captured to the United States, in exchange for medical supplies and toiletries.

Churches began sneaking parishioners who expressed their anger at the regime and were at risk of arrest onto the ships, among them Abu's father, who was both an active member of the Methodist Church of Holguín and an opponent of the regime.

One day in late May 1963, Abu's father told his son and daughter-in-law that the time had come. Ama's mom helped her bundle up her infant daughter's clothing. Abu and Ama were allowed to take what they were wearing and two more outfits in their suitcases. They set out for the 10-hour drive to Havana from Santa Lucía. They said goodbye to their families not knowing if they would ever see them again.

At the Port of Havana, government officials checked the passengers for jewelry before they boarded the ship, Morningside. "They didn't take any of our stuff, but what were they going to take?" Ama recalls. "We didn't have anything."

Ama and Abu joined the rest of the passengers in the boat's hold for the overnight journey to Port Everglades in Fort Lauderdale. Their daughter was given a cot. That night Ama lied on the floor beside her baby and tried to sleep. She couldn't.

As the ship set sail, Abu called to her, insisting she had to see something. She followed her husband topside and saw the crowds covering every inch of the Malecón, waving their white handkerchiefs in the distance as the sun set over Cuba. It was then that Ama knew they were never coming back.

Christy Piña *is a journalist from Miami, Fla., who covers lifestyle and entertainment. Christy interned at The Hollywood Reporter and covered sex and dating for Elite Daily. Her work has been featured in Her Campus, Irving Publications and WUFT News and she aspires to become editor-in-chief of a major magazine one day. When she's not working you'll find her binge-watching her favorite TV shows, reading, journaling and hanging out with friends.*

Sarah Sackler, Inc.

Sad Sacks, Inc.

IF I close my eyes, I can go back to the lazy afternoons of my childhood, when my grandmother was still alive. She'd run her fingers through my hair as I rested my head in her lap and listened to stories about her life. What I wouldn't give to get that time back now.

It had been a week since she died and my family started the unhappy work of cleaning out her house. As we made our way through each room, we found boxes and boxes of photographs squirreled away in drawers and the backs of closets. One snapshot caught my eye.

It was taken in the summer, likely the 1950s. My grandmother, who looks to be in her 20s, is at the center of the photo. She is seated at a small table surrounded by other young Armenian women and their mothers. She's looking almost wistfully into the camera.

The scene drew me in and I wished I could have joined her. I wondered what they were talking about. I flipped the photo over, looking for a date or anything that might provide some answers about who these women were to my grandmother. But what I saw instead was a note written, unmistakably, in her handwriting. It read *Sad Sacks, Inc.*

My grandmother had a girlish sense of humor. I had a hunch that the phrase was poking fun at these young women, who might have been stuck inside with their mothers on a beautiful summer day.

I wanted to hold onto this photograph and so I snapped a picture of the front and back on my iPhone before returning the photo to its box. Over the coming year, I found myself looking at the photo often, pulling it up in the moments when I wished I could call my grandmother.

If I could, I would have asked her why she had written *Sad Sacks Inc.* What about this moment, these women, this day, compelled her to do it?

∞

My grandmother's Armenian name was Anahid, but she went by Anna. She immigrated to the United States from Aleppo, Syria with her mother, father and

44

three brothers in 1937 at the age of five. Her mother, Victoria, survived the Armenian Genocide and fled Turkey for Syria as a little girl. Victoria met her husband, Azar Azarian, in Aleppo.

Azar came to the United States before the 1915 genocide, where he married and had a son. Both his first wife and their son died of unknown reasons. After their deaths, he traveled to Syria in the hopes of finding a new Armenian wife. Victoria had also been widowed, and her son, Stephen, was the same age that Azar's son would have been. They married in the 1920s and remained in Aleppo until 1937 when Azar took his new family back to the Armenian enclave where he had lived in America.

The family settled in an apartment on Elm Street in Lawrence, M.A., where Azar had secured a job at the Pacific Mill Company. Over the years, Victoria and Stephen would also hold jobs at the Mill. The Azarians attended Holy Cross Armenian Apostolic Church in Lawrence, where Azar served as a deacon.

Anna and her brothers graduated from Lawrence High School. In the yearbook, Anna stated that she had ambitions to become a private stenographer and that her hobbies included bowling. The bowling came as a surprise to me, but my grandmother would hold many secretarial positions throughout her life.

∞

Anna grew up surrounded by Armenians, who had begun coming to Massachusetts in the late 19th century, settling in industrial towns. Watertown, Lawrence, Arlington and Boston were filled with Armenian families. The sounds of Armenian folk music could be heard in the streets when churches held bazaars. Families grew grapevines in their backyard to make *yalanchi* (stuffed grape leaves) and frequent picnics carried the aroma of middle eastern spices.

Her best friend was Rose Aznavorian — that's Rose sitting in the far left of the photograph. Rose's father, Avedis, owned a grocery store in Dorchester and the family lived in an apartment above. Their fathers, my relatives insisted, had both come from the same village in Armenia.

"We came home one day and there they were in our living room," Rose would recall years later. "It was almost like they were right off the boat and ours was the first place they came."

Neither family owned a car and so they would take turns traveling to each other's homes by bus. Anna and Rose became the sisters neither had.

∞

There was Anna and Rose, and then there was Adrina Boyajian and Grace Haroutunian, whom Rose had befriended when she joined the choir at Holy Trinity Armenian Apostolic Church in Boston. In the photograph, Grace is seated in the far right and Adrina is seated between her and Anna.

The group called themselves "the sisters."

The church was the center of social life for young Armenian women. For children whose parents had survived the genocide, Rose would say, it was like "an umbrella of protection." Her parents were overprotective and granted her little independence, outside of the church and the choir. "The sisters" did everything together — church, picnics and, eventually, Saturday night dances. They dreamed of one day owning an apartment together, where each girl would have her own floor. And when they married, it would likely be to young men they met at a dance sponsored by the Armenian Church Youth Organization.

The most popular performer at the time in Massachusetts was Artie Barsamian, King of Armenian Swing. If Barsamian was set to perform one of the dances, the girls knew the music was going to be "outstanding," recalled Adrina. Barsamian was reimagining Armenian music that was more Americanized than the traditional folk music of their parents and grandparents. Partygoers danced the *Shourch Bar*, a line dance growing in popularity, set to Barsamian's music.

The girls stayed close until they started getting married. Then everything changed.

∞

A popular tradition among Armenian women is coffee ground readings. An older woman said to have a talent for reading fortunes takes your empty demitasse cup in her hands. She swirls the remaining coffee grounds in the bottom before flipping it into a saucer. After the grounds run down the edges of the cup, she'll read the messages that she finds in the patterns of the drip.

I've heard about these readings, but I never had one done myself. My grandmother used to tell me that her mother had a knack for it and performed readings frequently for guests. If you were a young, unmarried woman your fortune was guaranteed to be something to the effect of, "There is a handsome and rich Armenian man in your future."

While their grandparents and parents may have had arranged marriages, young men and women of the 1950s had the freedom to choose their spouses — so long as they married fellow Armenians. The arranged marriages after the genocide were about survival as much as they were about tradition. If word got around that a young man in America was looking for a wife, families would send their daughters from Syria, Iran, Lebanon and other countries to be married. Men like my widowed great grandfather, Azar, would even travel to Syria to find a bride.

Anna was, as best as anyone in the family could tell, 23 years old on the day this photo was taken. And she was single, as were the other young women sitting at the table. Adrina told me that the pressure to marry, and to marry an Armenian man, was never explicit. But it was felt. Women were, on average, 20 years old when they married in the 1950s, putting "the sisters" behind the curve.

Perhaps this was the reason my grandmother thought of them as *Sad Sacks Inc.*?

Anna and her friends were raised in homes where their mothers cooked traditional foods, and where they spoke the Armenian language. Children raised in the United States had two halves — their ethnic Armenian and American halves.

Soon "the sisters" would begin to leave the comfort and insularity of their community to start new lives as wives and working women.

∞

Adrina, the youngest of the group, was the first of "the sisters" to get married. She married Eddy Tututunjian, Grace's cousin, and they moved away to Troy, N.Y.

Grace, who was a few years older, was next. She married Abraham Bozian when she was 32; a cousin had introduced them. The couple stayed in Arlington, as did Rose, who would never marry and who worked as a medical secretary before becoming a teacher.

Anna, meanwhile, started to grow apart from the group. Shortly after the photo was taken, she moved with her family to Albany, N.Y. Her father, Azar, had died of a heart attack in 1949 and the family opened a boarding house. Her brothers worked in a children's clothing store called the Wonder Shop. Anna worked as a secretary, and her new friends in Albany had last names like Behr, Kibbe and Schmitt.

She remained single until she was 33. At her brother Mardi's wedding she met a young Armenian man from New Jersey named John Zakar. Two years later they ran into each other one summer in Asbury Park, a popular vacation spot for Armenian Americans. They married eight months later and Anna moved to New Jersey, creating ever more distance between her new world and the one in which she had grown up.

∞

I'd like to think that my grandmother was ahead of her time, a modern girl who wasn't afraid to wait for love even if it meant marrying late. She held many jobs and helped support her family as a single woman. And while she kept her Armenian community close, she brought outsiders, *odars* — non-Armenians — into her world.

But I cannot be sure. Nor can I be sure whether *Sad Sacks Inc.* was a moment of self-pity at being 23 and unmarried. What I do know is that for the surviving women sitting at the table that day, the bond that came from growing up as they did endured long after they had married and moved away.

"It makes me happy that I had these times," Adrina told me. "Not everyone can say they had that life."

"These friends will always be friends no matter what," said Rose. "We are still bound to each other."

Close as they were, neither Rose nor Adrina could say why my grandmother wrote the phrase. But I have come to see that it does not matter. What I discovered was that there was a richness to her life, in her friends and in coming of age in a world where everyone ate the same foods, spoke the same language and shared the same tragic legacy.

The photograph I found and carried with me wasn't just a picture of my grandmother. It was a photo of another time, a vanished world.

Marissa Roberge *is a journalist from Fairfield, Conn., who covers arts and culture, women's issues and daily news. Prior to her journalism career, she worked in non-profit development. Her reporting has been featured in the Brooklyn Ink and she aspires to write for a major magazine or digital media company post-graduation. When she's not working, you can find Marissa exploring New York City's restaurant scene with friends or lounging on beaches, dreaming of clam chowder and oysters.*

The Last Sweet Shop

EVERYONE in my family grew up spending summers at our cabin on Grace Lake in northern Minnesota. It's a small, simple cabin built in 1937 by my great-great-grandmother. I always thought that if my soul resided in a physical location it would be there, somewhere between the dense woods, the long gravel drive, the garden and the memories.

I would walk up and down the cabin's long, pine-paneled hallway and look at the framed photographs. Among them are pictures of my family's tragic legacy: the sweet shop. It was called Black's Purity Sweet Shop and I grew up hearing about it, especially from my father who would fantasize that we'd all be millionaires if the family hadn't sold the shop.

It closed in 1961, the year my father was born. Through his inherited nostalgia, I came of age believing that if the shop had somehow stayed open, our family would still be influential and important — that we'd still have something that made us special.

I always wanted to know what had happened. What was this place my family had staked so much of itself on? Who started it and what went wrong? It was in that cabin that I first discovered what my family once had and what we lost.

∞

John Neal Black was supposed to be a florist. His father had been a florist. His grandfather had been a florist. The Blacks were flower people. But like flowers, they sometimes died before they bloomed.

John did not go into the flower business. Instead, he would head west to seek his fortune. He would find it in a distant city that was ready for a young man who dreamed big.

He was born in 1873 into a prominent Boston family of florists and horticulturalists. The Black family, originally of Scotch descent, had resided in the Boston area since before the Revolutionary War, and in the 100 years prior to John's birth, they had accumulated a degree of respectability and wealth. But, in 1880, John's father, William, died at just 29 years old. John's newly widowed mother,

Elizabeth, kept the family in Boston for four years after her husband's death so John could continue his education in the common schools. In 1884, Elizabeth moved the family to Minneapolis. At 11 years old, John was now the man of the family and so he began working to support his mother and two younger sisters.

Contrary to familial expectations, his first job was not in floristry, but in confectionery. John learned the confectioner's trade from J.T. Garland, the leading candy manufacturer in Minneapolis. John started with a humble salary of $4 per week — just over $100 today — and over the course of 10 years, he worked his way up. By the age of 21, John was travelling around the country to train with prominent candy manufacturers. He moved from Minneapolis to Chattanooga to Cincinnati to Lima, Ohio before finally settling in Grand Forks, N.D. in 1902. There he worked for a confectioner named H.K. Geist for four years before he set out to make his mark on his own little corner of the world.

At the turn of the century, Grand Forks had only been an established city for a few decades. Native American tribes, such as the Ojibwe and others from across the continent, had used the land as a crucial meeting and trading point for thousands of years. In the 1600s and 1700s, French colonizers took control of the land to use as a trading post for fur trapping. The French named it *"Les Grandes Fourches"* for its two intersecting rivers, which fork near the center of town.

American settlers acquired the Dakota Territory through the Louisiana Purchase and a series of wars and genocide against the Native peoples. In 1870, a United States Post Office was established in the new town of Grand Forks. When North Dakota was incorporated as a dry state in 1881, all the saloons and brothels moved across the river to the neighboring sister town, East Grand Forks, Minn. East Grand Forks became known as a "wide open town" where laws were lax and enforcement even more lax. The brothels were raided once a year when everyone paid a fine before resuming business as usual.

Both towns grew rapidly with the arrival of the Great Northern Railway, the Northern Pacific Railway and the University of North Dakota in the 1880s. The population doubled nearly every decade, and by 1900, the towns' combined population was around 10,000. In this landscape of rapid growth, Western expansion and controlled chaos where Christian family values fought against encroaching vice, John Neal Black began to build his dream.

John's first foray into business ownership came in 1907, when he opened a candy department in the local grocery store, Colton-Wilder Grocery Company. The endeavor was so successful that within a year, he was able to move to his own location in downtown Grand Forks. The first Black's Purity Sweet Shop was located next door to the Empire Theatre, the first theatre to come to Grand Forks. Here, John primarily sold homemade candy and ice cream, as well as popcorn to neighboring theatre-goers. The shop's prime location helped it become wildly popular. He hired his sister-in-law, Mary Boese, who quickly displayed her skill as a manager. Years later she would tell the Grand Forks Herald that "her brother-in-law was a good candy and ice cream manufacturer. But he would undertake twice as much as he could handle. The shop was small and when he had a big order for ice cream, there would be the big tubs and freezers with ice and salt standing around waiting for the truck. It seemed as if they were always wading around in that salty slush and constantly mopping floors."

But John Neal Black had his sight set on expansion. In 1915, he opened a second location in the Scandinavian American Bank Building that, at the time of its opening, was the pride of downtown Grand Forks and was featured on postcards. As John's business continued growing, this space became the flagship location of Black's Purity Sweet Shop.

Black's shop thrived in its new home. This was largely due to the efforts of Mary. Mary, the sister of John's wife Christina, never envisioned the life of a confectioner for herself. While John had defied his destiny of becoming a florist, Mary had always dreamt of being a florist. By the time the new location opened, Mary had saved all her money and was ready to get out of the candy business. She opened a floral counter in the new shop. But as John focused all his energy on expanding his enterprise, Mary was left to take over management of the shop's day-to-day operations.

John opened an ice cream manufacturing site in East Grand Forks, where he produced and packaged ice cream to be distributed and sold in grocery stores across the Midwest. He opened Black's Bakery in East Grand Forks. He made plans to open a candy counter in The New Grand Theatre, which began construction in 1918. He had married well. Christina was the daughter of one of Grand Forks' earliest settlers. They had nine children, one of whom died at the age of four.

John and Christina hosted parties at their home for local community organizations. He operated a booth selling soft drinks, candy and cigars at the North Dakota State Fair. He donated candy prizes to local competitions. He opened a doughnut kitchen next to the shop in the Scandinavian American Bank Building. He had his hand in dozens of business ventures at once, and his efforts were well-known throughout the community. But under pressure to keep the booming business running smoothly, Mary's flower counter quickly withered and died.

"Mr. Black had a flair for promotion," reported the Grand Forks Herald, "and was so busy with the new that the old was left to Mary to bring order to the picture."

Black's Purity Sweet Shop expanded steadily. John put in a soda fountain and added chairs and tables to serve ice cream and cake. Due to "a constant demand for sandwiches," according to the Herald, "a sandwich counter was put in.

People dropped in and lunched on sandwiches and ice cream and wished they had soup. So next it was soup." Now developing into the restaurant business, the shop quickly needed more space for its growing clientele, so John rented out more space within the grand new building. He bought an Edison "Century Model" phonograph for the shop's new Japanese tea room. The Herald called it "the handsomest phonograph ever to be brought into the state of North Dakota."

While Mary ran the shop's flagship location, John maintained his other storefronts where he sold candies, baked goods, ice cream and confections. He had risen to prominence in the Grand Forks social and business scene, and his endeavors were regularly featured in the Herald. A profile of him as an influential business owner was featured in a 1917 book called "North Dakota History and People: Outlines of American History." His shops were described as "attractively equipped [to] bring to him a liberal patronage…His business has been developed along legitimate and substantial lines and he employs in the factory and his stores thirty people on an average. He has always concentrated his efforts along this single line, has studied the wishes of the people and has manifested a spirit of initiative in bringing forth new products in both ice creams and in confectionery. All of his goods are standard products and his success is indeed well merited, being the logical and legitimate reward of his earnest, persistent effort."

The shop's reputation for quality was unparalleled. Out of 137 confectioneries inspected for cleanliness in the state of North Dakota in 1916, Black's Purity Sweet Shop was one of just two shops to receive a perfect score of 100 points. As a testament to their cleanliness, all staff — bakers and servers alike — wore uniforms of pure white linen. The women wore winged white caps reminiscent of WWI nurses. Nearly every edition of the Herald featured advertisements for Black's Purity Sweet Shop.

"Yes! You Can Get Them at Your Grocers

BLACK'S PURITY

HOME-MADE

BREAD AND PASTRIES

None better

If better could be made, BLACK would make them"

"After the Show, Follow the Crowds to BLACK'S Purity Sweet Shop

Where you will be served with Ice Creams, Sundaes, Sherberts, Parfaits, Refreshing Drinks, and Appetizing Lunches"

"Don't fail to drop in now any time, for we have added another qualified dispenser to our fountain. This insures you quick and excellent service at all times"

"Cocoanut Candy Week at

BLACK'S Purity Sweet Shop

We will place the following kinds on sale at

Special Price 30c Per Pound

Cocoanut Caramels

Cocoanut Kisses

Cocoanut Wafers

Cocoanut Klondyke

Cocoanut Sour Kraut

Cocoanut Bon Bons

Cocoanut M. M. Bells

Cocoanut hand rolls, chocolate hand dipped"

Family legend has it that in 1918 or 1919, John took out a $50,000 bank loan — equal to nearly $1 million today — to continue expanding his empire. But, just as business was booming, tragedy struck.

John Neal Black had suffered from diabetes. The illness, however, had never slowed him. But in 1919, at the age of 46, he died suddenly from complications related to the disease. Two years after his death, insulin was discovered as a life-saving treatment for diabetics.

The business was left to Christina and Mary. The widowed Christina had eight children at home and Mary was already managing the business. The empire that John Neal Black had built was left to his sister-in-law to save.

Mary's friends and family all told her to sell. She faced a tough decision: sell the business she had grown to love, that had become such an integral part of her community? Or take on the heavy task of ownership while she still had her own child to raise? "You know," she later told the Herald, "there are times when you just have to sit down and think and think, then decide for yourself what seems to be the right thing."

The right thing to do, she decided, was to keep the business alive. My family tells me she convinced the bank to let her take over John's loan, which she eventually paid off. In 1919, a woman owning a profitable business was rare, but Mary was a rare lady. She had been an actress, a vaudeville performer, a hostess who was said to be a friend of Harry Houdini and the life of any party. Now, she was also a female business owner at a time when most women were relegated to the home and not yet guaranteed the right to vote.

∞

The first thing she did was sell the ice cream manufacturing leg of the business. She kept the flagship location of Black's Purity Sweet Shop as well as Black's Bakery in East Grand Forks. But two years later, in 1921, tragedy struck the family again when Mary's husband died suddenly. She, too, was now a widow and a mother, and between her and Christina, there were nine children to raise and a booming business to maintain.

Mary forged on. As the nine Black children grew older, they began to help out in the shop as dishwashers, busboys, waitresses, bakers and delivery drivers. When John and Christina's eldest son, Bill "Tiny" Black was old enough, he took over Black's Bakery, likely sometime in the late 20s or 30s. They called him Tiny, my Grandma Susie says, "because he was very big!"

As for Mary, Susie says, "She was the matriarch of the whole family. If you wanted something, you went to Auntie Boese. If you had to talk about a problem you had, you went to Auntie Boese. If you needed money, you went to Auntie Boese."

Mary was close to her grandson, Rev. Robert Sorenson, or "Bouncy" as my family calls him. Nearly everyone in my family has a silly nickname — there's also Hunky, Smudgy, Peachy, Tula, Rickie Tickie, Hossy and Teever. Bouncy grew up in a big farmhouse with Mary and his mother, Viola — Mary's only child who had also been widowed at a young age. "It was not like a normal grandmother-grandson relationship," Bouncy says. "We grew up together."

Bouncy started working as a busboy in the sweet shop when he was in junior high, in the mid-1940s. "She was a good boss, but she was tough," he says of his grandmother. "She was strong." He says she treated her staff well and always hired people who needed work. Every year at Christmastime, she'd take everyone out to dinner at a local restaurant called Whitey's. "It was always a fun time," Bouncy remembers. "The staff enjoyed it a great deal." She would still bus tables, waitress and do dishes everyday alongside her staff. "It was the kind of place that served the working people in the town," Bouncy says.

Sometime in the 1940s or 1950s, the Bank Building went through renovations and Black's Sweet Shop moved a block and a half down DeMers Avenue. Its interior looked almost identical. It was a big space, with long glass casings full of enticing treats flanking the entrance. There was also a long counter with red vinyl stools. On either side of the shop, there were long rows of red vinyl booths. The soda fountain was behind the counter under hanging pots and pans and rows of numbers telling you what station you were sitting at. By the 1950s, all the waitresses had shed their pure white linen and were now uniformed in matching pink dresses with white aprons.

My great-aunt Doris, who married into the Black family, recalls Grand Forks in the 1950s when she was in high school. She'd cruise around town with her friends. At lunch, students from her school would walk to the sweet shop to hang out. I can hear her smiling through the phone as she tells me about the glory days, listening to records and drinking Coca-Cola, which "was a big deal back then." They'd munch on éclairs, candy bars, sundaes, nutty chocolate candies, lemon pie, coconut cream pie, cakes, cookies and fresh-baked glazed doughnuts with a scoop of ice cream in the middle. Even in the 1950s, she says walking into Black's Sweet Shop was just like "walking back in time." And on weekends, she says, "we'd go with my grandpa and grandma who lived on a farm and we'd sit in our car and watch the people go by on the sidewalk. It was a busy place."

My Grandma Susie, the granddaughter of John and Christina Black, grew up in the sweet shop too. She remembers "sitting at the soda fountain drinking a Coca-Cola, or sometimes a malted milk. And when you sat up there, that was a big deal to a little kid, you know." Susie worked in the sweet shop when she was in high school. Mary, she says in her thick Minnesotan accent, "was such a good example. And she did it in such a sweet way, but you knew doggone well that she was the boss, but she treated you very well."

Like her brother-in-law, Mary became a prominent person in Grand Forks. She was elected Oracle of the Royal Neighbors Club, Vice President of the Modern Brotherhood of America and committee member of the North Dakota Federation of Business and Professional Women's Clubs. She chaperoned local dances, hosted elaborate holiday dinners, donated to churches and served treats at town events. The Herald made a point of noting when she left for a week-long business trip to Minneapolis and again when she returned.

Her success made it possible for seven of the Black children to attend college. Together with Black's Bakery — which was eventually run by John's son Tiny — it also provided the money for Christina and Tiny to build beautiful homes next door to each other and to build the cabin at Grace Lake. "She wasn't greedy. She wasn't rich," Grandma Susie says. "But she kept the business going so that the family could survive."

∞

Then, one day in 1961, Mary was getting ready for another day of work at the sweet shop. As she was putting on her nylons, she fell back onto her bed and died. Her family knew something was wrong when she didn't show up for work. Even at 81 years old, she still worked an eight-hour day.

Her death devastated the family, especially her grandson, Bouncy. It's been almost 60 years since Mary's death but talking about it now, Bouncy still sighs deeply and says, "It was certainly sad for me," adding, "It was tough. It was hard."

After 54 years, Black's Sweet Shop died with Mary. The family members who remained in Grand Forks were too busy with their careers and their families to keep the shop going. My Grandma Susie exhales as she says, "I don't know, it just wasn't feasible. It was time."

I asked her if she was sad when it closed, and though she wouldn't admit it, I wonder if she reminisces, as my father does, about what would have happened had the shop stayed open.

"You know, I think as a family we all expected it," she replied, "and we all kinda knew that they were keeping the shop open for Auntie, that it was time. I think quite a few years before that, they thought it was time, but nope, doggone it, she'd be up and going to work. The shop was her life."

She continued. "The [Black] women were very hard-working women. Period. It was just bred in you. You just go get it. You just work. We were taught to grow up like that. The women were widowed young and they had to work and survive everybody, so they were hard workers. They just were."

Growing up, every time I thought about the sweet shop closing, I felt an immense sense of loss, a loss I couldn't even claim as my own — it was an inherited, nostalgic loss, passed down from generation to generation. Thinking about it gave me the kind of creeping sadness you feel when you hear a distant train bellowing its horn in the middle of the night — the hollow sound coming from somewhere both far and unknown, yet close enough to hear.

We still have the cabin at Grace Lake, which I was named after. This summer, I will visit the cabin again. I'll run my fingers across the beige vinyl kitchen counter, which was brought over from the sweet shop after it closed. I'll hear the loons calling their lonesome song over the water at night. I'll walk up and down the long wood-paneled hallway, knowing what we lost, but also what we kept.

Grace Eliza Goodwin *is a journalist from Seattle, Wash., by way of Chino Hills, Calif., who covers racial and social justice issues. Prior to her journalism career, she worked in arts nonprofit fundraising and event planning. She also spent seven years managing Seattle's largest bed & breakfast. After graduating from Columbia Journalism School, she plans to continue living and working in New York City. When she's not reporting or producing audio pieces, Grace can be found taking long walks through Central Park, making cocktails and studying French.*

They that turn many to righteousness shall shine as the stars forever and ever.

Daniel 12:3

Rev. Zion H. Berry – 1839-1903

Organizer of the Corner Stone Missionary Baptist Church 1889,
and was its first pastor.

The Mystery of Haven Creek

ZION HALL BERRY stared into the camera. He had dressed for the occasion. He had slicked back and parted his hair. He rested his arm on a pile of travel cases to keep from moving. The date is unknown. As best anyone can tell it was in the late 1800s, by which point Berry had lived a life of wealth and prominence as a man of color in the enslaved state of North Carolina.

I came across this family photograph by chance. The more I stared into his gaze, the more I wondered who this mysterious man was. How did he become the forbidding-looking man captured in this photograph? How did he rise to prominence at a time when, all around him, people of color were in chains?

Berry was a pastor and a landowner. He was educated. He traveled across the state to preach. His accomplishments were chronicled in the local newspapers.

How did that come to be?

∞

He was born in April 1830 in Camden County, N.C. Little is known about his early life. At the age of 20, he was still living in Camden County with his mother Lucrecia and his sisters, Mary and Nancy. In the coming years he would marry and with his wife, Nancy, have three daughters and two sons. How he learned to read and write is unknown, as is much else about his life leading to and through the Civil War. All we know is that he and his family lived as free men and women.

The record became clearer in 1880 — 15 years after the end of the war — when Zion Hall Berry was 50. By this point, he owned his own home, a farm where he resided with his family. In 1881, he became a member of the Roanoke Missionary Baptist Association. He spoke so regularly that his absences were noted in the local paper. He wrote often. His penmanship was distinctive for its slender, coiled and cursive letters.

In 1889, he became reverend of Cornerstone Missionary Baptist Church on Roanoke Island. Perhaps this photograph commemorated the event. He established several other churches in other counties across the state.

Legend has it that he was a tough man, as the look in this photograph suggests. He was said to be stern and pious. In addition to their family, the Berrys could afford to take in four children from other families who, like the Berry children, were taught to read and write. There was also Dennis Harvey, a 40-year-old boarder, whom the census identifies as a farmer. The Berry home sat on 27,000 square feet of fertile land in a place known as Haven Creek.

∞

When I asked people in my family how it was that Berry had enjoyed this rare status, I was told that that was just the way it was. But that answer did not satisfy me. Why was he free when so many were not?

The answer came through understanding something about Berry's home. It turned out that he did not buy his house. He inherited it from his father who had, in turn, inherited it from his father. The privileges he enjoyed did not begin with him. In fact, they began long before he was born.

The oldest deed in Robeson County — located a few miles off the coast — was signed by King George II of England in 1732. It allotted land to two individuals, Henry Berry and James Lowrie. Both were men of color. Among the families that rose to prominence in Haven Creek before the Revolutionary War were the Lowries and the Berrys. But their origins were far different than those of the enslaved men and women brought to North Carolina.

When the first English settlers arrived in 1587 on the coast of what would become North Carolina, they encountered a local population they called the Croatan Indians. Bit by bit, the Native population assimilated the English, so much so that eventually, their colony vanished. Simply put, they mixed. And so was born the legend of the Lost Colony of Roanoke.

The truth is, the colony didn't really disappear. Some Croatan Indians adopted the same names as those settlers. Their descendants remained and benefited from a privilege their counterparts rarely had: they were the direct descendants of that first colony and so intimately tied to an American myth. The state of North Carolina later granted them special status, one below the Whites but above the Blacks. So it was that the Croatans were considered American citizens before 1865.

Over the years, free people of color with Native American roots often mixed with Black or White people in Haven Creek. Many children of color on Roanoke Island were born from a White mother and a Black father. Children would keep the rights of their White mothers. The Union Army attacked Roanoke Island in 1862 and succeeded in taking the island from the Confederacy. The Native American population in Haven Creek approached 6,000 at that time. Like most Native Americans in the region, they claimed Cherokee ancestry, as did Berry.

Roanoke Island, where the Berry house stood, was known as a haven for runaway slaves. If you could get on the other side of the water, you were safe. You had reached Haven Creek.

By the turn of the 20th century, the Croatans were said to have abandoned all Native American customs and habits, among them language and last names. Not only did they speak perfect English, but they used words that had become obsolete in most English-speaking countries. The word loving was pronounced "*lovend*," father was "*fayther*" and man was "*mon*." Language was a core part of the tribe's heritage.

The Croatans were allowed to have separate schools of their own. These schools were different from those established by the government to force Native American children to assimilate. The Croatans and their descendants could choose their own teachers and benefit from an education on their own terms, free from government intervention.

∞

Berry and his counterparts shared an ancestry that allowed them to become citizens, landowners and, for some like him, wealthy and influential members of society. Although they claimed Cherokee heritage, their geographical location protected them from displacement. President Andrew Jackson had signed the Indian Removal Act in 1830, which resulted in the genocide of thousands of Native Americans across the nation, including the Cherokee.

The Croatans' status was also a racial one. They were considered a separate race in the eyes of the state of North Carolina. But there was a growing sense that the Croatans bore what some observers saw as a hatred for Black Americans. Was this supposed hatred merely a way for the Croatans to secure their land and their rights? Or did some Croatans enslave Black people whom they considered chattel? Berry's will lists chattel among his assets but there is no indication of what this meant. Census records of the pre-Civil War South would list names of slaves. There is no such record for Berry.

Zion Hall Berry died in June 1903. He received a traditional Christian burial. The estate remained in the family for many years after, as Berry had wished. His wife Nancy inherited all his assets. She later passed those on to their son J.C. Berry. J.C and his brother Edward remained on the farm after their father's death.

∞

Over a century after Berry's death, the mixed heritage of Haven Creek's population is still visible. Some descendants of Berry and his peers today identify as African Americans. Some of them still part their hair in the middle, wearing it in twin braids. Their skin is light with reddish undertones. Their eyes are sometimes gray. A hundred years ago, these physical attributes helped the federal government identify who the Croatans were in Haven Creek. Today, some of those physical attributes remain the same. My grandfather, Henry, was an African American man who had Native blood running through his veins.

Every few summers in the late 1970s, my grandfather would drive his two children to Haven Creek to spend time with their grandparents. One night, he told them, "We have to go see the play of 'The Lost Colony.' It's the story of our ancestors." They drove to the ocean and sat in an amphitheater overlooking the water. The play began before sundown.

They watched a boat floating on the shore. The wind brought the taste of sea salt to their lips. The English set foot on the land that would become America. They had their first encounter with those who lived on Roanoke Island. Henry's daughter, my mother, was captivated by the play. But she didn't fully understand how it related to her family. "If it's the story of our ancestors," she asked, "why are we sitting here in the audience?"

The answer sat a few miles from the shore, where Haven Creek Baptist Church still stood. Zion Hall Berry was its first reverend. There it was, our past and our connection to him.

Kyra Alessandrini *was born in New York City but grew up in Paris, France. She covers arts and culture, mental health and issues of race and representation. She has worked as a writer and reporter for Radio France Internationale (RFI). Upon graduation, she plans to broaden her scope of reporting by focusing on race and social media culture. When she's not reporting, Kyra travels as much as she can. She loves to explore new cities and discover new cultures.*

The Road from Crystal City

I grew up hearing stories of my great-grandfather, who had first come to America from Mexico as a picker and would rise to prominence as a man of influence and respect. His name was Daniel Vargas.

My mother remembers him packing her and her six siblings into a station wagon filled with food and taking them to the migrant camps along the west coast of Michigan to deliver supplies. He was the first Latino man to sit on the Community Relations Commission for the City of Grand Rapids and was even appointed by Governor Romney to head the commission on migrant labor, later receiving an award from Pope John Paul II for his work.

These are some of the stories that became our family lore. But I'd always wanted to know more — how did Daniel Vargas, one time *matadero* ("slaughter-house") worker turned migrant farmer turned railway worker, become the man in this photograph in the suit and tie?

∞

He was born on June 7, 1907 in San Pedro, Coahuila, Mexico to Carlos Sifuentes Vargas and Maria Lozano Delgado. He was part of a large family and, as some recalled, one of 18 children. The family was said to be of Mexican and French heritage, which may explain his sharp hazel eyes and light complexion. Fortunately for Daniel, his aunt operated a prestigious private school, allowing him the opportunity to receive an education free of charge, a gift that would alter the course of his life.

Over 600,000 Mexicans entered the U.S. between 1910 and 1929; Mexican laborers were in high demand and were being heavily recruited to work in the fields of South Texas. Two of his brothers had already made the move to a town about 50 miles from the border, Crystal City.

Daniel arrived in 1926, two years into the surge in spinach production across the Winter Garden Region, an agricultural area made up of Zavala, Dimmit, Frio and LaSalle counties. Formerly dry, arid and filled with mesquite trees, the land wasn't irrigated until the late 1890s. In 1905, two land developers purchased the

Cross S Ranch, selling plots of the 10,000-acre farm and designating the area as Crystal City.

The San Antonio, Uvalde and Gulf Railroad, allowed crops to be shipped out across the country, further spurring the agricultural boom. During the 1923-24 season, for instance, over 900 carlots of spinach were shipped across the country. By the time Daniel made it to Texas, that number had surged to 2,500 carlots.

The farmers needed pickers and so it was Daniel's arrival that marked a peak in migration to Texas. Between 1920 and 1930, the population of Crystal City grew from less than 1,000 to over 6,000. The immigrants lived in shacks with dirt floors, many packed into a room. Sanitation was poor and diseases ran rampant, among them, tuberculosis.

Migrant workers across the country traveled with the seasons, following the crops. Those who made Crystal City their home base picked spinach, cotton and onions in the Texas winter and, come spring, headed north to states such as Wyoming and Montana to work the sugar beet fields.

The 1930 Federal Census shows Daniel living with his brother Nestor, Nestor's wife Consuelo and his younger brother, Carlos. Next door lived Guadalupe Pequeño, a recent widow, living with six relatives and her two-year-old son, Magdaleno Rodriguez.

The woman herself was said to be able to pick cotton more than any man on the field. Her husband Refugio Rodriguez died the year before, falling ill with pneumonia after a trip from Wyoming to Texas in a winter storm. Her first child died in 1926 when she was just four months old.

Sometime in the next two years Daniel Vargas left Texas to return home to Mexico, only to cross the border again at Laredo in 1932. That same year he married Guadalupe Pequeño against his family's objections. She was a widow and had already conceived two children and was therefore regarded as impure. He ignored them.

Spinach was continuing to boom in the self-proclaimed "Spinach Capital of the World," ironically, during the same period Popeye the Sailor — *I'm strong to the finish cuz I eat my spinach* — rose to fame. A cartoon of Popeye, Olive Oyl and Wimpy on their way to the Crystal City Spinach Festival appeared in the Llano News to highlight the city's first annual edition in March 1936. The following year a Popeye statue was erected in the town.

By 1938 Daniel was working as a labor contractor — a man in a suit. Contractors were Mexican migrants who would recruit laborers and then serve as their supervisor in the field — weighing crops, dispersing payment from the landowner and handling affairs between workers and farmers.

Meanwhile, racism grew across the country. Life on the road, traveling from farm to farm, made racist attacks increasingly part of everyday life. They were denied service at restaurants and often turned away from convenience stores. Mexican families continued to till the soil, powering the country's agriculture industry, yet they were unable to reap many of the benefits — a reality that would still trouble Mexican-Americans almost a century later.

Thousands of workers from Mexico came to Crystal City. And when the harvest was done, the Vargas family, like so many others, moved on, following the crops. But by then, many Mexicans were beginning to migrate north, finding stable employment opportunities in factories or working on the growing railroad system, which would provide Daniel Vargas' pathway.

World War II brought even more opportunity for Mexicans in America. In 1942 the government launched the Bracero program, which encouraged Mexicans to come to the United States as contract workers — especially for farm work. Wages were low and working conditions were poor.

Meanwhile, some of Guadalupe's family left for Michigan. In 1941, the Vargas family found its way to Grand Rapids, Mich., where some of Guadalupe's family had recently settled. She started working at St. Mary's Hospital and Daniel began working for a railroad company. There weren't many Mexicans living in West Michigan, which for a bright, educated and eager young man with a growing family, could mean opportunity.

∞

In the years to come, my great-grandparents helped create Our Lady of Guadalupe Chapel at St. Andrew's, where three generations of the family would attend school. As a member of one of the few Mexican families in the city, Daniel joined the Sociedad Mutualista Circulo Mexicana, providing translation services and taking numerous Mexicans to get their driver's licenses. He even became good friends with future president Gerald Ford, a congressman at the time.

Daniel worked until 1962, until crippling arthritis made work impossible. He did, however, continue his political work and activism. In fact, it was after retirement that he threw himself ever more into this work. For all of Daniel's accomplishments, however, it is understood in our family that the driving force in his life was Guadalupe, the woman his relatives had not wanted him to marry. She was quiet but stubborn and it was she who held the family together, which would include 22 grandchildren and 10 great-grandchildren by the time of his death in 1992.

Daniel died one week after the couple celebrated their 60th wedding anniversary. In time, Guadalupe grew ill and moved in with their daughter, Maria. She refused to be taken to the hospital, threatening all of her children that she would die if they sent her there.

She began having dreams. She would look out the window from her bedroom and see Daniel drive by in a car, but he never stopped. In the next dream, Daniel turned and looked at her. And finally, he stopped.

Allison Arnold *is a journalist from Grand Rapids, Mich., who covers food, culture and social issues, with a focus on giving a voice to underrepresented communities. Her work has been featured in Grand Rapids Magazine and Women's LifeStyle Magazine and she has plans to write a book of her own one day. Allison has a love for outdoor adventure such as hiking and kayaking and enjoys traveling, cooking and exploring restaurants.*

Not Quite Born in the U.S.A.

THERE is nothing more Irish than the telling of lore. My parents say a summer day in 1985 isn't old enough to be considered legend, but folklore is never decided by those who live the tale. At the beginning of any folklore is memory. It's one thing to recall parts of great days, but remembering an entire day from dawn to dusk with clarity and detail is something entirely different. As they sat with their friends in the historic castle's field, my mom and dad had no clue they were living out their own lore.

My parents remember every detail of June 1, 1985. The day stood in contrast to the typical gray of Dublin life back then and played out like a piece of modern legend as they recounted the events to me 35 years later. Everything about that day was a rarity. It began with a blank check left in a car and ended in a pub filled with bellows of "Born in the U.S.A." sung in thick Irish voices. The weather was hot. The beer was flowing from plastic cups. My dad was wearing tin foil over his nose and goofy short shorts exposing his pasty white skin. Bruce Springsteen was looking out over the sea of 95,000 Irish people burning under the sun, all waiting to witness the Boss play his first concert in Ireland at Slane Castle.

Bruce Springsteen isn't simply intertwined with my parents' immigrant story; he was the catalyst of it. There was an unspoken bond forming with Springsteen and his music that would lead my parents on an adventure to uproot their lives in Ireland and move to the United States in search of a new one. This bond, however, began a decade before the concert, before my mom and dad knew each other.

∞

In the 1970s and 1980s, it was common for young adults to leave Ireland for summer work. There were little to no jobs available in the country. Ireland only broke from the centuries-old mold of financial depression in the 1990s, during the Celtic Tiger period. While my dad, Brian, went off to various European cities, such as Copenhagen and Amsterdam, my mom, Stephenie, ventured to the East Coast for two summers in a row and worked in Asbury Park, N.J. — Springsteen's local haunt.

She bumped around seasonal jobs, serving stints as a waitress in different family-owned boardwalk restaurants and cafés. It was here that she learned to love America, even if it was a naïve version. She ordered piña coladas every night she went to a bar. There were no cocktails in Ireland. She went to an African American wedding. People didn't dance like that in Ireland. She met people from different places with different viewpoints. Some people she met were bad, no doubt, but it was the good people who filled her vision of the U.S.

One woman, in particular, stood out to her. She was the mother of my mom's then-boyfriend, Bruce (not Springsteen). As opposed to the conservative Catholic parents of Ireland then, who would have loathed the sight of Stephenie appearing from their son's room in the morning, this Polish-American woman treated her with a candid kindness from the moment they first met. Though Stephenie can't remember her name, she remembers her blonde curly hair and refreshingly warm smile. At 21 years old, she felt for the first time as though she were being treated as an adult by someone her senior.

"Is this what Americans are like?" she thought.

During her first summer in America, in 1974, Stephenie claims to have seen Springsteen play at the Stone Pony, the music venue now bestowed with legendary status among hardcore Springsteen fans, back when he was an emerging local boy. Her American friends dragged her to the show where hundreds of people were packed into the small space. Since pogo dancing was the fad at the time, the audience was jumping up and down throughout the concert, obstructing her 5-foot-2-inch view as she stood near the back. She couldn't really see what was happening on the stage, but she felt the electric buzz in the room.

Springsteen's first performance at the Stone Pony was on September 8, 1974, so unless Stephenie stayed in the States past then, it wasn't the Boss she saw that summer night. Perhaps this is an editing of memory from 46 years ago, or maybe she did stay in New Jersey through mid-September. The art college she was attending in Dublin typically began later in the month. She can't remember. She maintains she saw him, maybe as a guest performer sitting in with another band, as he often did in those days. She also maintains the sense of irony that she got to see Springsteen, in the most famous of Springsteen places no less, years before Brian, who had to wait a decade to see his hero live.

She did, however, actually see the Boss on tour the following year. Back in Asbury Park for the summer, Stephenie joined her three American work friends to a hyped-up, sold-out show in New York City on August 13, 1975. In a now-defunct cabaret theater in Greenwich Village called The Bottom Line, Bruce Springsteen and the E Street Band lashed into a set to promote his highly anticipated third album, "Born To Run," scheduled to release in just over a week.

Within months, he was on the magazine covers of Newsweek and Time as the new face of rock and roll. The 10 back-to-back shows at The Bottom Line burst with classic Springsteen sweaty electricity and became another source of legend. Brian was also able to feel and hear the vivacity of Springsteen perform, but through staticky cassette tapes on the north side of Dublin.

Brian's relationship with Bruce Springsteen's music began when his buddy, Declan, gave him a vinyl copy of Springsteen's first album, "Greetings From Asbury Park, N.J." He listened to it on repeat on a record player in his small boxy room at home on the northside of Dublin. At that point, it was the summer of 1973 and four months later, Springsteen's second album, "The Wild, the Innocent & the E Street Shuffle" was released, just in time to further fuel his building fan fever. Brian ran to the record store downtown that November to get his hands on the album as soon as he could. He listened to that record so much, the needle wore it out.

He spent the next decade getting his hands on anything Springsteen-related he could find. He read about the emerging American local boy-turned-rockstar in the New Musical Express magazine and listened to his vinyl records on repeat, waiting a few years at a time for each new album to come out. To supplement in the meantime, Brian bought concert bootleg recordings from a seller on O'Connell Bridge downtown above the River Liffey. The cassettes were stacked inside a shabby cardboard box and decorated with handwritten track listings and pixelated paper prints on the front. Springsteen once famously yelled at a 1978 concert, "Bootleggers out there in radioland, roll your tapes!" The quality of the live recordings was usually scratchy and terrible, sometimes hardly audible, but it was the closest Brian could get to experiencing the electricity of his musical idol performing.

He got an even closer glimpse at what the magic of Springsteen live was when the Boss appeared on a 1979 episode of "The Old Grey Whistle Test," a British TV show for non-chart music that "provided many seminal musical moments for its dedicated viewers," as the BBC put it. Brian was one of those dedicated viewers; it was his gateway into many of his now favorite artists, from Springsteen to Jackson Browne to Crosby, Stills & Nash. A young Springsteen sliding across the stage on his knees and jumping on the piano while performing the energetic song, "Rosalita (Come Out Tonight)," was unlike anything he, a young Dublin man from the rough side of town, had ever seen.

He loved everything about Springsteen. He spoke to Brian. It was the most exciting thing he had ever heard in music. It all spoke to him — the songs, the lyrics, the magazine write-ups of concerts, the cheap live recordings, the distant videos from a country across the ocean, everything. It was the most important music to him as a young adult.

When I asked why, he said in his Dublin-turned-Californian accent, "There was an awful lot of shite around, a lot of disco. But he was authentic."

∞

By the mid-80s, Brian and Stephenie were six years out of art college and had moved in together. They lived with a third roommate, Pat, in a quaint rented townhouse in Raheny Village on the north end of Dublin. Brian was working as an industrial designer and detailer at a shopfitting company called Dolan Brothers out in the peripheral suburb of Swords. He spent most workdays sitting at a large drawing desk surrounded by rulers, pencils and colored pens to sketch store interiors — think an architect's workspace. He wasn't making that much money, but enough to be comfortable. Each week he would be handed a wage packet in the form of a brown envelope with cash inside, £140 a week, he thinks.

He was content enough in his job. His coworkers, Seamus, Sean and Michael Dolan, were full of inner city Dublin wit and fun to be around. The fact that he had a job, alone, was something to be happy about. Ireland's economy, as it had been for decades before, during and after the fallout of the Irish War of Independence ending in 1921, was struggling. There weren't enough jobs for the population and a lot of people were living on the dole, particularly in Dublin. Securing a job in any capacity meant you were in good shape. If you lost your job, prospects of finding a new one were dismal, lest you be highly educated, and only the already wealthy were.

Stephenie worked at an advertising agency in Dublin, called Kenny's, as a production assistant producing TV ads, setting up shoots and logging videotapes. She took the 46A bus into town to an area near Georgian houses every day. Her desk looked over a canal.

As a way to reinvigorate the economy by developing more skilled workers in the 1980s, the Irish government paid people to take technical extended education classes as an alternative option to being on the dole. The state agency was called *An Foras Áiseanna Saothair*, the Training and Employment Authority, and referred to as *FÁS*, which translates to "growth" in Gaelic. Stephenie took a fast track course in video production and editing that led to her job.

In their late 20s, Stephenie and Brian weren't well-off by any means, but they had more disposable income for things like concerts and weekend trips to the west of Ireland with their friend group than before. Unlike most of their friends, Brian had a car. He drove it back to Dublin from his two and a half years working at a construction site in Germany. The Renault 5, a miniature and boxy French car, was bright green. Its steering wheel spun 360 degrees around and was on the left like American cars, the wrong side for being in Ireland. At some point in the car's life, he accidentally kicked his foot through the floor of it. He continued to drive it around with a hole showing the moving road beneath him for maybe a year before it finally gave up and died.

Brian, Stephenie and their friends would take the car on weekend trips around New Year's to the countryside of County Clare, where they would rent out cheap flats in small towns, drink at local pubs at night and take nice walks during the day. Other than that, fun for them was simply having Friday and Saturday night pints at their go-to walking distance pubs, the Green Dolphin and the Manhattan Lounge. Sometimes they would make the drive to the Cock Tavern in Howth, a rainy seaside town north of Dublin, where they would sit around chatting for hours and joining in on live Irish trad music.

There was nothing to do except go to the pub. Stephenie said "that's where life was." Nothing much beyond having a steady job and going to pubs for fun was expected out of young adults in Ireland. But they were happy. This was all they really knew. They would do just as their parents and grandparents and great-grandparents had: work, have a few pints, sing a few songs and go on day to day.

∞

June 1, 1985 began with panic. Stephenie woke up just before 7 a.m., hours before anyone was planning to arrive. Out for a pint the previous night, she had lost a blank company check somewhere in the city. She thought it was maybe in a car parked outside of the advertising agency. And so she sped off on her yellow moped to the southside of Dublin to retrieve the check and save her employer, and herself, from disaster.

When she arrived in the parking lot, she was relieved to spot the check through a window sitting in the back seat of the company car. The problem was that she didn't know what to do with this information. In an age before cell phones, she had no way to contact any coworkers and didn't know how to break into a car. Instead, she hopped back on her moped and hoped for the best. Luckily, the day had distraction in store for her.

She looped her way back home, passing through a part of town with butcher shops on just about every block. Whizzing past the butchers, she pulled over and stopped inside a spot famous for its sausages to grab breakfast for the group, all of whom would be arriving soon after she got back to the house. She walked up to the counter and ordered a *bartley*, a Dublin slang term for a wrap-up of whatever breakfast items the butcher had that day. It would typically look something along the lines of sausages, rashers (thinly sliced Irish bacon) and black and white pudding (blood sausage with oats mixed in). When Stephenie got home, she and Brian fixed up plates of the butcher's bartley, eggs and toast. Aiden, Rose, Phil, my uncle Brendan and aunt Mary were expected to arrive any minute now as part of the concert convoy.

Brian drove some people in his tiny Renault 5 to the concert. Phil drove the others. While everyone else packed basic ham and cheeses for the show, Phil brought spinach and brie sandwiches. He always brought eccentricity to the group dynamic. Once, he brought with him a coffee maker that plugged into the car's cigarette lighter. As it heated up, it began to fill Brian's car with smoke. Brian started to worry that the whole car would catch on fire, so Phil simply tossed the machine out the window onto some Dublin city road.

It was a rare Irish hot summer day. The essentials were packed: blankets to sit on, flaggans of Bulmers cider, hats to protect their pale Celtic faces from the sun and, in Brian's case, tin foil to cover his nose since his hat alone wouldn't cut it. Everyone in the crowd flaunted skimpy summer outfits, sun-screen slathered skin and drenched tops from sweat, of course, but also booze.

The Belfast Telegraph reported 95,000 people in the audience, which stretched down the green of Slane Castle in County Meath, about an hour and a half out from Dublin. There are major cities in Ireland with populations less than the number of fans who showed up to see Springsteen. It was such a massive event that it earned a mention in the Boss' 2016 autobiography, "Born to Run." Springsteen wrote that "the crowd closest to the stage were deeply into their Guinness and dangerously swaying from left to right. They were opening up gaping holes amongst themselves, as audience members by the dozens fell to the muddy ground vanishing for unbearable seconds 'til righted once again by their neighbors."

Seeing the hoards of sweaty and rowdy fans sloshing around in the mosh pit that emerged right in front of the stage, Springsteen considered canceling the show altogether for fear of disaster. He thought someone was going to die and it would be his fault. It would end up on the Sunday news across the globe the next day. But the crowd began to calm as the music played, and the Boss carried on.

Though Brian didn't know it at the time, this fiasco may have been the reason he wasn't as in awe of the performance as he thought he would be, as if Springsteen was off his game. Brian specifically laid off the cider, because he didn't want the first concert memory of his idol blurred by drunk goggles. But when it came to the show, the first half fell slightly short of his expectations. He dared not tell anyone at the time, so as to save the purely elated mood, but he didn't sense the pure unhinged sound and performance he had come to know from bootlegs and magazine reviews. He would see better shows in years to come, the next in 1988 at the RDS in Dublin, but that didn't stop this concert from taking up a significant place in his mind.

For the rest of the group, the concert was a party, a whole day affair of drinking and dancing. They were content spreading out in the grass further back from the crazy hoards of fans up at the front. Brian had made everyone arrive at the venue two hours early right when the gates opened at 3 p.m. to snag a good seat, so they were sitting nearer to the stage than most of the audience. But he wanted to be closer.

"Everyone else was there for a good time, but I was there for my hero," he said. "If he had come out on stage and farted I would've loved it."

When the tickets were first announced earlier in the year, Brian trekked into town to a record store and lined up for hours before the sun came up to make sure he got some. He wasn't going to miss this. He made sure of it. Each ticket cost £15 and he left with the maximum number of tickets in his pocket. They were blue with silver embossed lettering.

Springsteen came out on stage in a yellow and maroon striped polo shirt and a pair of black jeans, both pieces of clothing close to exploding from his flexing macho American muscles. His wood-bodied Fender Telecaster was hanging from a leather strap strung over his shoulder. The setlist was one Springsteen fans would die for these days. The first set began with "Born in the U.S.A." and thrashed its way through to "Thunder Road," Brian's favorite, 12 songs later. Set two started with a costume change — a rarity for the Boss. Now flaunting a sleeveless black denim vest over a loose fitted tee, Springsteen lashed into "Cover Me" then "Dancing in the Dark" then "Hungry Heart." Brian screamed "I'm On Fire" at the top of his lungs as the sun lowered over the stage and the castle. By the time Springsteen and the E Street Band exited the stage, they had performed 27 songs.

The night wasn't yet over for the gang when the concert ended. A hater of "chockablock" traffic, Brian pulled out from where he had parked and headed for the backroads behind the castle. After a short time in the car, they spotted a small pub called Ryans of Gormanlough around the bend of a road and dove inside for a pint. It was packed with people from the show. Everyone stayed until closing before heading to Scanlan's chipper, because the whole place rang with leftover buzz from Slane. A makeshift choir full of Irish country folk swung their pints of Guinness in the air as they loudly slurred the words to Springsteen hits, "Born in the U.S.A." the loudest of them all.

∞

Stephenie felt like she had blinkers on living in Ireland. The country was in a recession. It had been for as long as she could remember, but she really felt it after losing her job at the advertising agency in 1986.

Brian decided he wanted to work on his own as a freelance contractor, so he quit his job with Dolan Brothers. It didn't end up working out as well as he had hoped, because of the worsening economy, so money for them as a couple was getting tighter.

One bright spot in Brian's life was music. He had dreams since he was young of being a musician, and it kept up through his 20s. As a teenager, he bought a 12-string acoustic guitar, or rather his dad paid for most of it, and learned how to make it talk. Later, he'd own a brown Music Man electric guitar. Brian taught himself chords and fingerpicking patterns quickly over time. He would listen to his favorite artists like Neil Young and Bob Dylan and follow along, or buy sheet music from record stores downtown.

In the late 1980s, he occasionally played the acoustic guitar in a four-person cover band. Singing songs by Simon & Garfunkel and Crosby, Stills & Nash, they would perform in pubs for the price of free drinks. Brian, at one point, even auditioned to be the singer of a classic rock and roll band, but he knew he wasn't what they were looking for. He felt more connected to acoustic singer-songwriter music. Brian has always been musically driven, everything from sonics to lyrics, its escapist quality something he needs in his life even still today. He once had a far-flung dream that moving to the U.S. might give him an opportunity to pursue music.

When Stephenie heard news announcing a Green Card lottery organized by the American government, she decided to apply for Brian and herself.

These Green Cards became known as Donnelly Visas, named after Irish-American U.S. Congressman Brian Donnelly, who proposed the idea amidst an illegal Irish immigrant crisis. The lottery was supposed to distribute 20,000 immigrant visas to people from 162 countries selected randomly, but the Irish were the most successful. Irish applicants ended up receiving over 60 percent of the entire allocation of these visas worldwide. Oddly enough, a quarter of the visas awarded to Irish citizens remained unused.

Their first application letters were mailed to an office in Washington D.C. and Brian and Stephenie were sent back assigned lottery numbers at separate times under their separate names. To their surprise, they received numbers just one digit apart.

"This is uncanny," Stephenie thought, "as if it were meant to be."

She was the one that convinced Brian to apply because she knew they were both looking for something better. It was a mix of seriousness and romance of a different place, as well as the offerings of America and an adventure drove them. They had a history of trying new things and traveling, having worked in Germany for two and a half years and Israel for six months together. The U.S. would be a continuation of that. It wasn't an easy decision, but both of them knew the world was much bigger than Ireland. In Dublin, most people didn't seem to have the ability to see outside their own neighborhoods.

Stephenie recalled the freedom she felt those two summers on the East Coast. She knew firsthand what the U.S. could have in store for them. Brian, on the other hand, turned toward Springsteen for an idealized image of America, and he yearned for it. Springsteen's songs often told stories of disparity and tough lives, but they also spoke of hard work, opportunity and hope. Anywhere in the U.S. would be less stagnant than life in Ireland, and Springsteen sang of the promised land.

Each time they sent in more documents requested, they had to wait longer periods for the next steps. By the time their visas were approved, Brian and Stephenie had married, moved into a house in Marino and were expecting a baby.

In the summer of 1988, not long after their wedding in May, they had to travel to the U.S. within a specific three-month period to have their Green Cards validated. They stayed with Buzz, Brian's step-cousin, on Long Island.

The trip would also serve as their honeymoon, so they went on a pilgrimage to Asbury Park. They took a bus from Port Authority in New York City down to New Jersey. Stephenie was pregnant with my older sister and wore an oversized leafy Hawaiian shirt with a yellow skirt and white canvas Keds. In a solid aqua tee, patterned short shorts and white with black striped Adidas sneakers, Brian took pictures posing in front of famous Springsteen local landmarks, such as Madam Marie's white psychic shack on the boardwalk.

My parents returned to their newly bought house in Dublin, had my sister in October and then made the permanent move across the Atlantic to Mountain View, Calif. the following May of 1989. They only planned on staying for two years.

∞

In the photograph, my parents are poring over the Born in the U.S.A. Tour program, its big glossy pages filled with album and concert photos and bios of the band. Bruce's favorite color was listed as a white sport coat and a pink carnation, his hometown as under the boardwalk and birthdate as way back when.

The program sits in our living room now. The whites of the American flag-striped front and back cover have yellowed a bit. Last summer over a few gin and tonics my dad told me he'd leave it to me in his will. I laughed.

Springsteen occupies an oddly important space in my own life. I've been to five Bruce Springsteen concerts — the first one when I was in fifth grade. I've waited for hours in the pouring rain with my dad outside of the Oakland Coliseum with our general admission tickets to win the "pit" lottery. We stood in the second row at that show, and I've never seen my dad so filled with kid-like joy. I'm his official concert partner, always just us two. It's almost as if he tried to indoctrinate my older brother and sister before me with the magical ways of the Boss, but it only finally paid off and clicked with me. My dad denies any such plans.

Brandon Weigel once wrote in a 2016 concert review in the Baltimore Sun that "writing about a Springsteen concert as if it's a religious experience is basically a tired cliche at this point," and that's probably true. But the connection here is so obvious, it would be a shame not to make it.

In Irish myth, the Hill of Slane is known as the place where Saint Patrick lit the paschal fire that introduced Christianity to Ireland. It's only fitting that this was also the setting for my parents' folktale and the day they remember every detail of. If Springsteen preaches from a steeple in the church of rock and roll, he was a saint to my parents and they became converts that evening, whether they recognized it or not.

Now, over a late April backyard barbeque in California, as my mom lays out the wine glasses on the table, my dad's playlist shuffles to "Glory Days" from "Born in the U.S.A.," the tenth song on the setlist at Slane.

Claire Fox *is a journalist from San Jose, Calif., whose writing focuses on the intersections of gender, race, technology and culture. She has served as a senior staff writer at The Johns Hopkins News-Letter, a guest reporter at The Yonsei Annals in Seoul, South Korea and an editorial intern at Tokyo Journal. Upon graduating from Columbia, Claire aims to eventually work as a foreign correspondent for a major newspaper or magazine. In her spare time, she can be found reading books in hip cafés, petting cats and eating Korean food.*

83

Revolution Road

DARREN SEALS stood in the middle of a growing crowd of mourners outside the Ferguson Police Department. His eyes were hooded beneath a black Chicago White Sox hat as he watched the precinct's doors, waiting to see what the police would do. It was nine in the morning and people from all over St. Louis County had flocked to Ferguson. Seals, who was 24, observed, angry and still. He was being watched too.

Mathis Robinson watched him through his camera lens. He had been struck by Seals' silent rage, which was loud in the language of photography. So loud that Robinson was startled when Seals finally spoke.

"These signs don't mean shit to them! When they get mad they blow shit up," Seals cried out. "When we get mad, we march!" The crowd turned toward him. They lowered their signs and voices to listen as he spoke with increased urgency. "They just gonna keep killing us," he said. It was time for them to burn the city to the ground.

Robinson was a college student when he took the photograph of Darren Seals that would end up being disseminated across the country. Robinson did not know the name of the man whose photo he had taken, nor anything about him. It would take a year and a half before he began to learn who Darren Seals was, and why he was in Ferguson that day, raising his voice in protest. Seals would soon be dead.

∞

Ferguson was poor, Black and overseen by a majority White police force. Its police officers had been captured on videos beating Black citizens in the streets — choking one man in a wheelchair and pepper-spraying another already on the ground.

Seals grew up in Ferguson, in a neighborhood known as Castle Point. He worked at the local General Motors plant. When he was 18, he was arrested after getting into a fight with a police officer. He tweeted that he had "slammed" the officer on his head. He had also been shot on two separate occasions by unidentified assailants; the second time he was struck seven times.

Seals lived in downtown St. Louis in 2011 when Cary Ball Jr. was shot 25 times by police, not far from Seals' home. It is unclear from Seals' Facebook page whether he witnessed the shooting or came upon it afterward. Three years later, in 2014, Seals had settled in a neighborhood near Canfield Drive and not soon after, Michael Brown Jr. was shot on that very street by a police officer named Darren Wilson. Ferguson exploded with racially charged protests. And Seals, who by then had become an advocate against gun violence, was ready for a revolution.

"He had an electrifying personality and looking back on it now, I can say it all was destiny," says his friend Rodney Martin. He had met Seals in 2013, when Seals was recovering from his second shooting. "Every time he met someone, he left a lasting impression, whether good or bad. Some people he really pissed off and some really loved him to death." Seals, Martin and their friend Ron Gee quickly bonded over rap music.

Seals had heard a song Martin wrote that spoke about the killing of Cary Ball Jr. "He loved it. He asked me if I knew him, but I didn't. Darren told me he knew the family and the neighborhood Cary was from," Martin recalled.

Seals began thinking about the activism the three friends could achieve through music. They developed a code to live by: "Dimension of Ascension," or D.O.A.

"Initially, we were not a rap group, we were just three friends who rapped and hung out every day," he said. "Darren really cultivated that whole thing. There would be no D.O.A. without Darren Seals." Seals became the face of the group.

In July 2014, Seals and Gee held a gathering at a local restaurant to talk about activism and bringing change to Ferguson. "I don't mean activism in the sense of protests," Martin said. "It touched something inside of you that makes you want to stand up when something just ain't right." Then, less than a month later, Michael Brown Jr. was shot and killed.

Seals joined the protest outside of the Ferguson Police Department the following morning, and it was there that Mathis Robinson first saw him. Martin saw a change in his friend that day. "He was no longer the colorful, boisterous person we all knew in the streets," he said. "Now, he was the colorful, boisterous revolutionary."

∞

"I didn't know Darren before Ferguson. But I want you to know that he was a warrior," said one Ferguson activist, who, for privacy purposes, identifies herself as Nyota Uhura, a name taken from a Star Trek character. She first encountered Seals the day after the protest, during a march to Canfield Drive after the community vigil for Brown. "It was beautiful. It was the first time people all over St. Louis really stood up and stood together."

The protestors marched from the vigil in Canfield to West Florissant Road in Ferguson, where they were met by both Ferguson and St. Louis County police. Uhura called it a "kettle," blocking them from going forward and keeping them trapped by police cars so they could not leave.

"They weren't saying anything, just watching us and we were watching them. Some of them stood behind their cars like they were going to shoot us," she said. "We all started getting nervous because neither side was saying anything."

That's when she saw Seals. He was surveying the scene, and taking note of how they had quickly become surrounded by police. He didn't say a word. "We locked eyes, and that's the first time I really, really saw him. He stood out," she said. He looked angry rather than afraid.

Then the riots began. "The police car was set on fire. People were yelling. The police gave us no instructions, just let us react to being caged," she said. Eventually, the police had left. The riots continued and a convenience store was set on fire. Uhura decided to leave before the police returned with reinforcements. "Mike Brown wasn't the only thing that happened," she said. "He was just the straw that finally broke the camel's back."

∞

Seals became an organizing member of Hands Up Don't Shoot, a coalition that formed in the first few weeks following Brown's death. He led protests, spoke on community panels and organized marches, economic boycotts and clothing drives. He spoke with the young people of St. Louis. He was the one who held Brown's crying mother on the steps of the Ferguson Police Department when the crowd that had gathered there learned former police officer Darren Willson would not be indicted. "Darren was the heart and soul of our movement," Uhura said. Working together, Seals and Uhura used their social media platforms to promote community demonstrations.

Seals also had frequent public confrontations with Ferguson police. On July 25, 2016, he tweeted that "10 detectives pulled me and my 14 year old brother over, pointed guns on us, and told me 'Choose your enemies wisely.'" He recorded part of the incident on Facebook Live.

Uhura, Seals and other Ferguson activists had a tense relationship with the national organization, Black Lives Matter. "There's a large division in the movement and not many people know that. Darren Seals was not Black Lives Matter," she said. "The people doing the groundwork in Ferguson are not Black Lives Matter."

Seals often posted his feelings about the activist group on his social media.

He felt its organizers had hijacked the movement in Ferguson, turning the city into a symbol rather than a place where people needed change. He also began to question if there were donations to Ferguson and where the funds were going. He went so far as to slap DeRay Mckesson, a Black Lives Matter leader, in the face at a protest.

On the night of September 5, 2016, Martin went to his mother's house to eat dinner with his family. He remembers being so full that he went to the couch for a nap instead of heading home. "Darren called me, but I was full. I was sleepy. So I looked at my phone and said to myself, 'Oh, I'll talk to him later.'" Martin never called Seals back that night.

When Martin woke up the next day, he went to work as usual. "It wasn't until I was halfway through my day that I had got the news."

Seals was discovered in the early morning of September 6, in his car. He had been shot, and his car was in flames. By the time Martin had heard, all that was left behind were casings, ashes and a single car door. The killing remains unsolved.

People from all over Ferguson marched in Seals' honor the following weekend. On September 17, 2016, hundreds of people gathered at Greater St. Marks Family Church for his funeral, among them was Cary Ball Jr.'s brother. Organizations like the New Black Panther Party and the Michael Brown Chosen for Change Foundation were in attendance. The photo Mathis Robinson had taken two years earlier sat to the left of Seals' casket.

"My eyes gravitated towards his passion and my camera landed on him," Robinson said about the day he first saw Seals, in 2014. "I had no idea who he was." He would get a chance to see Seals from afar again at the Million Man March in October 2015. "He was sitting in the VIP area. I remembered him and his energy, instantly. I knew I took his picture back in St. Louis."

When he learned that Seals had been killed, Robinson was shattered. He remembers Seals saying, "'You can't keep doing the same thing and expect different results.'" Robinson recalled watching Seals through his camera lens. "And I heard the message behind that. It was out of love, but it was meant to start a fire."

Rachel Pilgrim *is a multimedia investigative journalist from Mount Vernon, N.Y., who covers stories concerning social justice, race and culture. Her work has been published on HuffPost, University of Cape Town's Varsity Newspaper and the Brooklyn Ink. She was also the host of Black Students United Radio, an undergraduate station at Cornell University. Post-graduation, Rachel plans on continuing her work with multimedia platforms and is excited about a future in podcasting. When she's not reporting, she can be found binging trash Reality TV and teaching her cat, Zora, new tricks.*

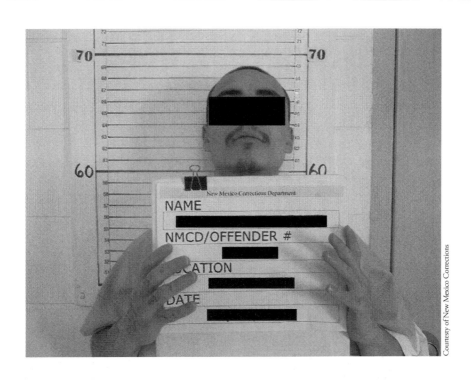

Finding D.

HE didn't have face tattoos when I knew him. He didn't have a shaved head. He certainly didn't have those rough eyes. Perhaps there was pain in them — I guess I never noticed, I was a kid back then, just like him.

Through the fog of childhood memories, I see a head full of curly brown hair and a soft, shy face that hid a rascally little soul behind it. D., whose family asked that he be identified by his first initial only, was never still — every single one of his teachers would love to tell you that. There was always something stirring in him — an energy of sorts released only through pranks, practical jokes or the occasional misdemeanor. But back then, we all committed harmless misdemeanors. Snowballs thrown at cars during winter. Disorderly conduct during summer. Ding dong ditches year-round. It was Brooklyn, N.Y. after all — teenagers got a high off it. So there was no reason to suspect those petty offenses would foreshadow a decade-long odyssey that would end in murder. But they did.

All pictures say something. Most whisper. Some converse personally with you. They reverberate inside, echoing off an old and buried life — tucked away under years gone by and memories long past, until they don't, flashing forward agile and violent, leaving more questions than answers in their wake.

The first time I saw this picture of D. in an orange jumpsuit, I felt sad, confused, surprised and guilty, oddly enough. As though I had failed in some way. I hadn't seen him in years by that point — he had moved back down to New Mexico where he was born, and we had lost contact. All I had left were memories of him, of that kid I had once known. In the photo, he's 22 years old and so very different. He looks cold, mature, pained. There's no innocence anymore. I wanted to understand that coldness — examine it in some way so I could answer the questions I had. But above all, I had to know: how easily could that have been me?

∞

D. had moved away from New York during his teens and was arrested for second-degree murder in Albuquerque, N.M. The years between had transformed him from spunky teenager to convicted felon. Understanding those years was the key to understanding why. A thousand miles away, while I finished my degree, fell in love, fell out of love, started and ended careers, D. became a murderer.

That time in his life was a mystery. When he moved, we lost contact with him. I only had breadcrumbs to work with. I followed them and started somewhere I thought was an obvious beginning: court records. Dry, uncut facts. With them in hand, I'd at least be able to build a foundation on which to position my understanding. In the end, they did little to that effect. They presented more confusion than clarity. They stripped the human away and left the caricature of a man. I knew those records told a half-written story. It was perhaps the only story about D. out there now — it printed the legacy of his life. But I believed that that half-finished story would help me chart the course of his criminal descent in detail, mapping the gradual change from innocence to guilt, discovering along the way what led him astray.

I started with the big one — his murder trial. According to records, D. had committed unpremeditated murder in 2013. He beat a man to death in Albuquerque, N.M.

The story goes like this: A friend of D.'s had been robbed while attending a house party. Her wallet and phone went missing, and she believed the owner of the house had taken them. The next day, she sought help from D. to retrieve the goods, believing a tough-looking young man would be more intimidating than a petite woman. D. said yes, recruited the help of another friend and went to the house to confront the owner. A scuffle ensued, a beer bottle was broken, and in the heat of the fight, D. badly beat the man. He died of his wounds shortly after. A heinous, horrifying series of events — all set in motion by a simple yes.

I'd eaten across the table from D. as a child. Played basketball with him. Awkwardly started conversations with girls, only to be brushed off along with him. We lived many formative years in each other's orbits. Never did I think I saw a killer. But the whirlwind of events following his yes told me either I had missed something back then, or he had changed, and I wanted desperately to believe it was the latter.

On that November day, two lives were ended — one by the knife, the other by the crime. The minute D. said yes, he sealed his fate. At the time that decision was void of any permanence or density — just one of a thousand decisions made during that week. That "yes" drew a line, forever separating his life before and after the incident. It's a reality people lazily call fate.

But I have trouble looking at D.'s yes as a matter of fate. That yes would shuffle him blindly through dusty New Mexico streets, under the searing heat of the southwest sun, into a small house and then finally onward to life behind bars. D.'s yes was not fate. It felt sinister and dark, more akin to a curse — one that was unintended yet self-inflicted.

The truth is the handiwork of that curse plays out a thousand times in court-rooms every day in this country. It begins and ends on the streets and in jail. That life can look less like a choice and more like a necessity.

I dug deeper into D.'s records trying to understand his particular curse. I did a thorough search of New Mexico's criminal databases, hoping there'd be some evidence documenting his slow and steady corruption. What I discovered began to paint a portrait of a young man caught up in a life he couldn't navigate his way out of from his first years in New Mexico. A young man arrested frequently, who stood trial with nothing more than a public defender and faced down judges with no support in the courtroom other than himself. One who had embraced criminal life quickly and without hesitation in his new home. In trying to understand D., I viewed his crimes unencumbered. What those records didn't show me, though, was everything else.

The years of documents I pored over followed a trail of offenses that led right up to that house and that murder. Those offenses increased in severity with time as D. seemed to fall deeper into a tailspin without the support, knowledge or op-tions to pull out of it. In those records, I began to see a counter-narrative to my own life. When D. was in court for burglary or drug possession, I was accepting awards for academic achievement. When I was on vacation in Ireland, he was trying to find someone to post bail.

D.'s first felony appearance as an adult was in 2009 in Albuquerque's Met-ropolitan Court. It was a place with which he would become very familiar in the years to follow. On May 31 of that year, he found himself at the mercy of the hon-orable Edward L. Benavidez in a grand jury trial on grand theft auto charges. D. was accused of robbing a car with a minor in tow as an accomplice. The jury voted for the case to move forward, and a criminal trial was scheduled for the next year. Bail was posted and D. was back on the streets. In that year between trials, D. would stand handcuffed in a courtroom many more times. Breaking and entering, burglary, distribution of narcotics, shoplifting and criminal trespass are just some of the charges he'd be brought in on. Many were dismissed for lack of evidence while others were not. Others led to minor jail time, enrollment in a community detention program and increasingly strict probation measures.

The first time the courts returned a guilty verdict was in October of 2009. While he reached that dark milestone, I was just starting my sophomore year at Adelphi University. That year, removed for the first time from the dingy corner stores and red-brick tenements of south Brooklyn, I would gain an ever-widening perspective on the world. For D. however, that year was a different beginning. He was charged with distribution of narcotics, to which he admitted guilt and copped a plea deal. His sentence was 36-days-time-served and probation. A month later he'd be found guilty of misdemeanor felony trespassing. Fifteen days after that, he'd be back in court for a minor shoplifting charge.

In January of 2010, his grand theft auto case finally hit the courts. It was a short one — D. copped a plea deal resulting in a sentence of 500 days in prison, minus time already served while on parole. Only days after his sentencing, I would be headed to a symposium on cultural diplomacy in D.C., courtesy of my university. He would be a few days into his first stint of hard time.

The crime and sentencing cycle continued all the way up until November 2013, when D. was arrested for second-degree murder. He was locked away and a lengthy criminal case proceeded. The final verdict came down in the fall of 2015. This time there'd be no bail, no parole, no community service. This time it was 40 years of prison time. On that day and in the days that followed, a jury would convict him, a judge would sentence him, a prison would receive him and a clerk there would give him a number: 742XX.

I can still see him clearly in my memories, full of life and energy, a mop of hair bouncing to and fro, navigating a burgeoning life. That was D., and I knew D. We all knew D. A hundred people will tell you so. New Mexico's Correctional Department didn't know him. They couldn't. They must have received and processed someone else. I mean, he certainly looked like D. Spoke like D., too. He was even just as short and scrawny as D. was. But, he wasn't our D. He was inmate 742XX, convicted of second-degree murder and sentenced to grow up and grow old in a cell.

The date of his appearance in court on those charges landed on a Thursday. I was tucked away behind a desk at my first real career, waiting for the weekend. A thousand miles away, behind barbed wire and concrete walls, my old friend D. was turned into a five-digit number. When I began this investigation, I told myself D. and inmate 742XX were different people. I dove so deeply into those records because I believed that whatever force had corrupted my friend in New Mexico would be obvious. It would tell me the story of a kid irreparably affected by broken societal structures. It would tell me how he dove headlong into an upstream current and was swept away forever. That was the story I wanted.

But that wasn't the story I found. D.'s move into criminal life was smooth and immediate in New Mexico. I wasn't reading the story of a criminal being made wholesale in New Mexico. There was something else afoot, something I hadn't considered when I formulated my original hypothesis. Whatever dark, spiteful spirit had sunk its claws into D. hadn't been lying in wait in New Mexico, separated from his life in New York by half a country. Maybe it was at work long before he left. Moving and manipulating behind that bright smile, it whispered with a sharp tongue, tainting his worldview right here in Brooklyn, right under my nose.

Maybe his prototype came to life right here, animating itself among the concrete and cinder blocks of New York City.

Maybe the pain I saw in his eyes when I looked at that photo for the first time wasn't new. Maybe it was always there.

∞

Whatever force it was that nudged D. and I down different paths, its origins were buried in the memories he created here, right at home. That force was a silent, glaring presence on those cold Brooklyn winters spent lobbing snowballs at luxury cars. It whispered in his ear during our pickup games in the park and colored how he perceived the world around him as we traversed it together for that short time. And whatever it was, it manifested outside of my periphery. D. hid it well.

When I first looked into that photo, I felt like I was seeing a new person in it. Not the one I had known. But maybe the truth was he had always looked like that. I was just too young and inexperienced to see him staring back at me. It was a troublesome realization to think that he suffered without notice. That I watched the beginning of his self-destruction, unaware that his mind was undergoing an unlicensed and unrequested renovation daily. D. had not killed himself. But he did end his life. To figure out why I had to seek out the memories that had influenced his outlook. The very ones that told him, so enthusiastically and so convincingly, that the world was frozen and bleak and barren, and in it, only cold spirits and hard hearts could ever survive.

I tried desperately to find him, but after weeks it became apparent that he was out of my reach. Amid the coronavirus pandemic, correctional departments across the country diverted resources to moving or freeing prisoners while simultaneously scrambling to ramp up medical services. By tracing digital records, I was able to track his last location down to a prison in southern New Mexico. After weeks of phone calls with employees who were just as confused as I was, I finally discovered that he'd been abruptly transferred out of state, to Virginia.

D.'s was an all-too-common case of a prisoner lost in a disorganized system with a long reputation of carelessly stewarding the incarcerated. Calling prisons across Virginia yielded only incorrect information time and time again. Eventually, annoyed staff summarily told me to call their headquarters, leave a message with a clerk there and wait for a response. That response never came, and how long it would take was anyone's guess. Even if it was sooner rather than later, the act of mailing a letter and getting a response — the only way to reach him at all, I was told — would take far too long in the midst of the pandemic. I was not about to give up the investigation, though, not when I was this close. And so I asked myself: if someone was trying to piece together my life without me, how would they do it?

I went in search of two different groups of people: those who had known D. personally and those who had known his immediate family intimately.

I realized I knew almost nothing about D.'s family. I seldom met them and can hardly recall him talking about them. And that was an odd thing where we were from. In a tight-knit friend group like the one we had, one's family was everyone's family. They were shared among us — someone's mother was everyone's mother, someone's siblings, everyone's siblings. Across race, religion, even language barriers, this was a fact that had always held true. But, most of us in that group had little to no interaction with D.'s relatives.

Stretched out across states, separated from D.'s life by stretches of time, I found those people I was looking for. Each one, from grandparents to teachers, had viewed D.'s life from different angles, telling their own parts of the whole story. It was one that started, for most of them, when an odd little family silently slid into their lives.

One autumn as the summer heat subsided and the school year began, D. showed up for the first day of elementary classes in New York with his mother, father and two younger sisters. They were embarking on what seemed like a long-overdue return journey. Many years prior, his mother had moved from New York to New Mexico, where D. was born. She was now returning home to New York with her young family. They set right to laying down roots, enrolling the three children in a small Christian school and attending a nearby church at the behest of D.'s maternal grandparents, Jerry and Nancy.

With church, school and a reunited family, they were poised to build a stable life. But just under the surface, things got messy. D. never knew his real father. The man that D. had referred to as such — the one who arrived with the family — was the boyfriend of D.'s mother. His two sisters were products of another one of his mother's relationships. Unorthodox arrangements aside, the family seemed to move as one, and went about busily solidifying their new life. They quickly made friends, found mentors and volunteered alongside their neighbors. Surrounded by new friends, his mother and her boyfriend even got married in their local church, hoping to raise their mismatched family as husband and wife.

From the first days of their new life, something was noticeably amiss. The children, D. especially, had behavioral problems in school. For him, it began with demerits for missed homework and — growing worse over time — culminated in a suspension for sexually inappropriate behavior a few months later. More than the rebelliousness of youth, it was an early sign that the new life they were pioneering was shackled to the past they tried to leave behind. Guided by their parents, the children began to withdraw, slowly but surely, from the community they once seemed so eager to join. Simultaneously, D.'s teachers say they saw gradual worsening in his behavior.

The catalyst of that change was a woman, who arrived on their doorstep on a winter day by bus then train, smiling as she forced her way into their lives. Around Christmas, an old friend of D.'s mother arrived from New Mexico. D.'s grandmother Nancy claims it was she that would unravel everything they had built, as she brought along with her the very demons that had pushed them to flee New Mexico.

I learned from Nancy that D.'s life had never been easy. As a child, he watched as his mother was consumed by an addiction to cocaine and uppers, using prostitution as a means to fund her habit. He saw this through young eyes, year in and year out. He'd be roped into it, too, when he was old enough. His mother taught him to steal, lie and manipulate. Her addiction was a struggle she had been unable to overcome. Her family's move to New York was likely in the hopes of finding greener pastures. It was meant to be an escape, a last ditch effort to save a drowning family. Just weeks after that friend arrived, D.'s mother abandoned her newfound sobriety, and with it, her new life.

D.'s behavioral issues were rooted in the brokenness of his home. And, as his newfound semblance of normalcy rapidly decayed, D. would get worse in the weeks and months ahead. Nancy and Jerry, for their part, knew all too well that their daughter had relapsed. They confronted her, hoping to salvage the progress the family had made. Instead, she got defensive. Soon after that intervention, the entire family would disappear just as abruptly as they arrived. Without so much as a goodbye to his grandparents, D. was ferried off, taken back to New Mexico.

The next time Nancy or Jerry would hear about D., it would be from child services. His mother returned to drug use and prostitution with renewed vigor and her husband abandoned the family shortly after. In no time, she'd follow suit, leaving her children and disappearing to her native Mexico, where she was never heard from again. After she left, the biological father of D.'s siblings took custody of his sisters but refused to take him. Forced into the foster system, D. was abandoned by everyone he had called a parent and stripped of the only siblings he had ever known. All before he finished elementary school.

Nancy and Jerry would move quickly to take custody, hoping they could provide him the home he'd been denied his whole life. In fact, Jerry was well-suited for fatherhood. He had made it his life's work to help people. A former gang member and drug addict, he had found God after being hospitalized from injuries he sustained during a street-fight. He dedicated his life to helping people who struggled in the same way he had, and over the years, he'd change many lives alongside Nancy. But as hard as they tried, and as much experience as Jerry had in dealing with the profoundly pained, he couldn't quite save D.

Trouble in school eventually led to petty crimes and shoplifting, and D. grew bolder in his rebellion against authority figures, including his grandparents. His grandfather's health began to deteriorate due to heart issues while D. was still in their care. Jerry's brother, who lived in New Mexico, stepped up and offered to take D. They agreed and said their goodbyes to D., not knowing it'd be the last time they saw him a free man. The arrangement in New Mexico lasted only a short time. D. continued his spree of petty crimes, eventually racking up a record sufficient to have him taken by the state once more and moved into a juvenile care program. From there, he'd bounce around from foster home to foster home until he was 18. With the freedom of adulthood he'd join a gang, get those face tattoos and four years later be found guilty of murder, the final conclusion to his long, painful story.

What I saw was a family that had descended on New York intent on carving out a new life. What I couldn't see was why. I couldn't see that, from the very start of his life, D. was being battered and bruised by circumstances he had no hand in creating. I couldn't see that inmate 742XX had been shaped by forces beyond his control from the moment he was brought into this world. And they didn't relent until the day he went to prison. I can't remember the last time I saw him. I can't remember what we did or what he said, although I'm sure it was profanity-laced and made me laugh till my sides hurt.

Every day as school let out, I went home to a house too small for all the people living in it. I went home to parents whose hair grew grayer with every bill they opened, whose faces grew more wrinkled thinking about the difficulties that went along with raising a family. But in the end, I went home to love. I went home to a place where children were children, and adults were adults.

I do believe D. went home to some type of love. But he also returned to a home where the pull of addiction was weighed against his welfare. He went home to a world where a child was forced to grow up too fast. And too often in his life, he had no real home to go to.

D. killed a man six years ago and he will suffer the consequences of that action every day. He committed a terrible crime, and so punishment had to be handed out. He took a loved one away from people who will continue to miss him sorely. It will affect decisions and steer their paths to some degree, just like D.'s memories steered him right to that doorstep.

Sometimes I find myself wishing I could scoop up the good fortune, the luck, the love I was given. With my hands full, I'd travel back to one of those cold, childhood winters to find D. crouched behind some bush, with a snowball in hand. I'd shuffle over to him, extend my hands in his direction and say, "Here, you. Take some of this and hold onto it tight. I never realized I had so much of it and you had so little."

Thomas Nocera *is a journalist from Brooklyn, N.Y., who writes about local city news, government and global affairs. His work has been featured in the Brooklyn Paper, Home Reporter, Aspire Magazine and Hartford Guardian. In the future, he hopes to focus on migrant crisis reporting as a fellow for the Groundtruth Project. In Thomas's spare time he likes to read and spend time with family and friends.*

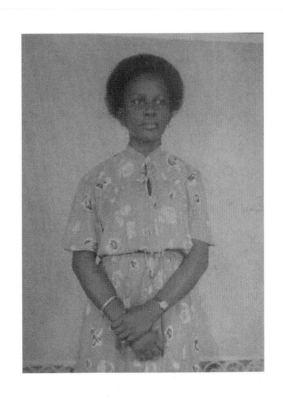

The Book of Esther

THERE was no doubt in my mind that my mother was the firstborn of nine children. Her eight siblings have been a constant presence in my life. She often shared her favorite childhood memories with my two sisters and me, the joys and challenges of growing up in a big family and her father's deep love for God which he made sure to instill in all his children. That is all nine of them, or so I thought.

One Saturday evening my mother and I were sitting in my small apartment having one of those nostalgic conversations. We were talking about her parents when she mentioned something in passing about her older sister being more of a daddy's girl than she ever was.

"They say she was always following dad everywhere," she said, a bit too casually.

"Sister? Mummy, you had a sister?" I asked, bewildered.

I was 22 years old and finding out for the first time that I had an aunt, the beloved oldest child of my grandparents.

∞

The year is 1960 and Samuel Osei and his wife, Hannah, have made their home in Djankrom, a small town in the Eastern Region of Ghana where they plan on raising their four young children. The family lives in an unfinished single-story house Samuel is building, with savings from his job as a construction worker. Their oldest, Esther, is eight years old. She is shy and introverted, the opposite of her six-year-old sister, Dorcas. Dorcas is full of energy and is often challenging their two younger brothers to a fight. Esther and Dorcas squabble from time to time, as sisters do, but they share a strong bond.

Samuel has just returned home for his lunch break, driving the short six minutes it takes him from his construction site to their home. Esther walks in shortly after, looking sickly. She has a tummy ache and when she couldn't keep focus in class, her teacher advised her to take the afternoon off. She would normally wait for Dorcas after school, but that day she made the 15-minute walk home alone.

It's a little after 4 p.m. and Dorcas returns home from school to meet her mother who is preparing her brothers for their evening bath. Surprisingly, Esther and her father are nowhere in sight. Within hours of Esther returning home, her temperature had spiked and she was vomiting incessantly. Samuel rushed her to their local hospital where she was eventually admitted overnight.

The following day, the doctors recommended that she be transferred to Korle-Bu Teaching Hospital, one of the biggest hospitals in Accra, Ghana's capital, for further treatment. It was about 10 a.m. the next day when Samuel set off for the hour-long journey, placing Esther gently at the back of his 1953 gray Benz. By the time they got to Korle-Bu, she could barely stand or speak coherently.

Samuel paced back and forth in the waiting room, unable to sit or calm his nerves. The night before he had tried to hold himself together so as not to alarm his wife and children. But he was terrified.

Now, one of the nurses appeared and handed him a list of drugs to purchase at a nearby pharmacy. She urged him to hurry.

He barely knew his way around Accra, having visited the city only once or twice in all his adult years. He loved his small-town life and was convinced the benefits of rural life far outweighed the advantages of an urban lifestyle. It was about 3 p.m. when he returned to the hospital with the prescription drugs, his eyes roaming the area in search of the nurse who had handed him the list. He spotted her talking to a patient and quickly walked over to hand over the medication. For a split second, it appeared the sense of urgency had left her eyes. She took the small white bag from him and led him to the doctor's office.

∞

That afternoon Samuel roamed the streets of Accra for hours before bracing himself for the drive back home. How was he going to tell Hannah and the children that her daughter and their sister was never coming home?

He could barely remember anything the doctor said after he told him that Esther had died shortly after he left the hospital to buy the medicine. He remembers struggling to stand as he listened. He also recalls falling to the floor in grief and tears. He wanted to scream and shout, but what was the point?

It was around midnight and Hannah rushed out to meet him when she heard his car pull in the driveway.

"How is Esther doing? Has she been admitted again?" She asked with a worrying look on her face when she realized Esther was not in the car.

"Yes, they are running some tests on her. I'll go back and check on her in the morning," Samuel answered reassuringly.

And so began a week in which Samuel hid Esther's death from his wife and children. How he managed to keep his pain and grief from them is beyond imagining. That week he organized some leaders in the community to perform a small burial for Esther in Accra.

How does a mother come to terms with the death of her child and her husband's lie? In Hannah's case, it seemed Samuel's decision to delude her was an act of love. He could only be protecting her. After all, in Hannah's eyes, Samuel could do no wrong. They would have four more sons and two more daughters. She would never visit Esther's grave.

∞

But Dorcas struggled to make sense of the loss of her sister. One day Esther was there. Then the next she was gone, never to be spoken of. Her parents hid Esther's photographs and belongings and eradicated every trace of her from their home. It was their way of coping with the loss and helping their children process the pain. But at what emotional cost? The uncomfortable silence made her loss even worse. Dorcas never saw her parents grieve and so never learned how to do so herself.

Dorcas was now the oldest and until the birth of her sisters was surrounded by six younger brothers. She missed Esther. But gradually the memories of her elder sister began to fade away. As a matter of fact, her parents made sure of that, just as they had intended.

Dorcas was thrust into the role of big sister and caretaker, responsible for helping her parents care for her younger siblings. But she also grew closer to her father. He was particularly strict with her, a fine line between teaching her to be safe and making her fearful of the world outside the confines of home. It was as if he was afraid of losing another daughter.

In the years to come, he would turn away numerous suitors. He would argue that she was not yet ready to leave the family nest. She didn't always agree with him, but like her mother, she loved him too much to fault him for it. Ultimately, she grew up to appreciate his strict parenting style, crediting it for her sense of duty, discipline and hard work.

∞

My mother and I share a bond; she's a friend like none other. But for years I challenged her overprotective parenting. A couple of years ago, when I was already in my late 20s, I decided to take a solo trip across Europe for my birthday. Living in Paris then, it was fairly easy to reach other European cities either by train or bus. As I shared the details of my trip with her, I sensed her fear and anxiety. She told me she would have preferred that I had discussed my plans with her before booking my trip. By then, I had learned the story of Esther and understood why my mother always seemed to approach life from a place of fear. It was all she had ever known.

∞

It's been almost a decade since that Saturday evening, and I'm still surprised when I recall the nonchalant way my mother mentioned Esther for the first time. Perhaps I shouldn't have been after I finally asked my grandparents about the daughter they lost.

My grandparents still live in the same house my grandfather built. They have been married for over 70 years now. I wanted to ask them about Esther but worried about upsetting them. I quickly learned that I had no reason for concern.

"What do you want to know?" my grandfather asked when I called.

I asked, "How did Esther die? Why didn't you tell grandma?"

"It would have been very difficult for her," he replied. "I wanted to protect her."

"How did you cope?" I asked.

"I was devastated," he said. He told me how he walked around Accra that night, how he eventually went back home and returned to the capital a few days later to bury her.

And afterward?

"Your mother," he said, "was always asking about Esther so we finally decided to hide everything so the children could forget about her and life could go back to normal."

My grandparents are devout Christians and see God's hand in everything, including the children born after Esther.

But I still wondered how my grandmother felt about her husband not telling her about Esther.

She replied that she understood. She was taking care of the other children, and so it was the right decision.

I asked my mother whether she had a photograph of Esther. All I had from that time was a photo of my mom. She said my grandmother told her she couldn't find one, that she was still searching for one. I suspect my mother does not believe her.

About a year ago, my mother learned that Esther was interred at Awudome cemetery, only a short 15-minute drive from our family home in Accra. My mother has lived there for decades, never knowing that her sister rested nearby. She has never visited her grave.

Oheneba Ama Nti Osei *is a Ghanaian-born French journalist and a Knight-Bagehot Fellow in Economics and Business Journalism at the Columbia University Graduate School of Journalism. She was previously the production editor for pan-African news organization The Africa Report where she managed magazine production in addition to her business reporting. An avid listener of audiobooks and language enthusiast, she is passionate about data-driven storytelling and women's issues.*

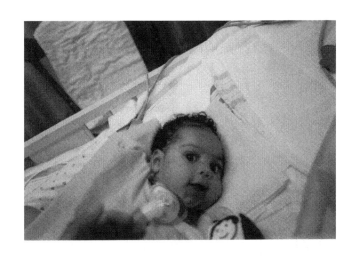

Itty-Bitty Hand

A COLLEAGUE of my mother's noticed it first. She had stopped by Nuttall Memorial Hospital in Kingston, Jamaica to see my newborn sister, Katya.

She pointed out a red spot behind Katya's ear and suggested my mother take her to the doctor to get it checked out. My mother agreed but then forgot. She was distracted by the new baby, and by the steady stream of visitors who came to the hospital to see her.

The year was 1999. My mother, Julie, filled out my sister's baby book, writing, "Most times I feel I can be a good mom. I know it's a lot of work; I just hope I'm up to the task." She had always taken meticulous notes on her life, documenting events and jotting out poetry in a leather-bound journal.

Her colleague visited a week later and pointed out the spot, again. "I totally forgot," my mother said. "I just thought the doctors had nicked her when they were delivering her."

My mother bought an antibiotic topical cream. In the baby book, she reassured her newborn daughter, "You had a little thing behind your ear, but we got antibiotics to clear it up." But the spot began to expand, getting bigger and redder. Her cheek swelled. My parents took her to the pediatrician.

"Oh," he said as he examined her. "Something we didn't see at birth."

My mother tipped forward, ready to fall out of the chair. "I had a child who was fine," she later told me, "and now I was going to have a child who was not fine." My father, Gordon, placed a hand on her shoulder.

He grew up in Mandeville, a country town high in Jamaica's mountains, where he and his brothers would trek through ruddy grasses, hunting birds. He had five siblings — four brothers and a sister — and lived in a home that was frequently strapped for cash. My father was a hard worker who shot to the top of his classes and was appointed Head Boy, all the while awaiting the day when he could move to the city for university.

My mother had a comfortable upbringing in Kingston. Her father was a university professor and her mother an official in the foreign service. Julie could often be found sprawled on the living room divan, sketching, in a half-pink, half-black pair of shorts. She was a gifted artist who occasionally painted scenes of Jamaica in acrylic or recreations of works by Picasso. She was thin and fair-skinned, with dark hair and eyebrows, and a smattering of freckles across her nose and cheeks. A gentle being, she was wholly unprepared for Katya.

∞

The doctor told my parents that Katya had "infantile hemangioma," a condition affecting around five percent of infants.

Hemangiomas are benign tumors consisting of blood vessels that form incorrectly and multiply without reason. The resulting birthmarks are bumpy and rubbery. The doctor opened a book and showed my parents images of babies with dramatic splotches of deep red on their faces and arms. Hemangioma was a topical condition, but the doctor had no idea how it would manifest in Katya. He sent my parents home. "Let's wait and see," he said.

Late one night, when my father was away on business in Cuba, my mother phoned the doctor.

"Listen to this child," she said, holding Katya to the phone. "Listen to her." Katya wheezed into the receiver with the raspy "*ee-ee, ee-ee*" characteristic of a child fighting to breathe.

He told my mother to take Katya to the hospital immediately. I was two years old at the time. My mother left me with my aunt and uncle and I fought them, not wanting to be separated from my mother.

At the hospital, the doctors put my sister on a course of steroids, which reduced the swelling, but her breathing did not improve. The doctor told my mother she would need to bring Katya to Miami. In Jamaica, they simply did not have an endoscope small enough to examine a newborn's throat.

My mother stood in line all day at the visa office in Kingston, rocking her wheezing child. Katya's loud, labored breathing drew stares from everyone in the office. My mother fidgeted beneath their unrelenting gaze, holding Katya tight against her shoulder. She thought, "Oh my God, this child is going to expire before we even get there."

"She was bones," my mother told me. Unbeknownst to my mother, Katya had been faced with a decision: eat or breathe. She had chosen to breathe.

Julie left Kingston for Miami with Katya in tow and only $2,000 in hand. My father was still in Cuba, so I was left with my grandmother. I climbed out of the crib in protest.

Katya was examined by Dr. Rafael Portela, a pediatric otolaryngologist at Miami Children's Hospital, who told my mother Katya needed an emergency tracheotomy. The nurses prepped her, but Katya was so dehydrated that they struggled to find a vein to insert her IV.

My mother leaned against the wall in the emergency room hallway, breathing hard. She dropped into a waiting room chair and called my father, whispering urgently into the phone, "I only have $2,000 and they're telling me it's $2,000 *a night.*"

My father hung up and set to work liquidating all of their assets.

∞

A red, bulging file marked "Katya - Medical" contains letters, documents and many, many bills. The tracheotomy cost tens of thousands of dollars. But most of it was written off by a charity program geared toward supporting the uninsured.

I had begun looking through the folder, and through emails, letters, photos, pamphlets, printouts, insurance forms and photocopied checks, trying to piece together what had happened to my family when Katya got sick. I had been too young to understand what was taking place around me. I knew only the little I was told, what I sensed I was not being told, what I could see and what I assumed was hidden from view. What really happened?

There was the money. I considered how different our lives would have been if the administrators at the hospital in Miami had not written off the hefty fee. The debt would have been devastating.

"I can't envision it," my mother said. "We would have still been paying."

And there was also the treatment itself, which would extend for years. Hemangioma of the face usually causes a temporary disfigurement and little else, eventually resolving on its own. But when it affects the larynx and the trachea, as in my sister's case, things become more complicated. An incision was made in Katya's windpipe and a breathing tube, or "trach," was inserted and secured by ties around the neck. "We didn't have a way, at that point, of controlling the hemangioma in that area," Dr. Portela told me.

Katya wore the trach for five years. I asked Dr. Portela about the resulting scarring. "We had to keep that string very tight," he said. "We would accept a scar on the neck [over] the risk of that tube coming out."

Katya underwent years of medical procedures following the first surgery: a procedure to remove the trach; a series of plastic surgeries to reduce and obscure the scarring the cotton ties had created; and speech therapy classes because the trach had inhibited her ability to communicate. Until she was fitted with a speaking valve, Katya spoke in short, expressive bursts made unintelligible by limited airflow and an enlarged lower lip, which weighed heavily on one side of her face.

The children at school would ogle the scars on Katya's neck and chin, asking if she had had her head bit off by a shark, or run over by a car. I would try, desperately, to shield her from their stares.

∞

In a photo taken just after the tracheotomy, a large hand — my father's — looms over Katya as he suctions the newly inserted trach with a plastic hose to remove mucus and secretions. Katya gives the camera a toothless grin. In her eight weeks of life, this was the first time she had smiled. My father shed tears of relief.

"For the first time in her short life, she didn't have to worry about breathing," my father later told me. "Can you imagine what it feels like if you're always struggling to take the next breath?"

My mother stuck a photo of me over the surgical table. "I wanted her to know she had a sister," she said. "I wanted you there."

My parents received a tutorial about how to change and maintain the trach. The staff made sure they were aware of the very real limitations of their home country — some services available at Miami Children's Hospital would simply be unavailable in Jamaica. But as it would turn out, this didn't make a difference. Like most parents of patients with a trach, my mother and father became immediate experts. "At some point, they become much better than the nurses at the hospitals," Dr. Portela told me. "In many cases, much better than the physicians."

My father became adept at changing trachs and was, according to my mother, the "king of suctioning." He trained the fleet of nurses charged with Katya's weekday care back home in Jamaica.

He told me that once, an IV was inserted into Katya's wrist, fixed in place with surgical tape wrapped twice. Her hand, clenched in a fist, was turning purple.

"It seems a little tight," my father had said to the nurse. He realized he would need to stand between his daughter and the medical apparatus working to save her: the harsh lights of the ICU, the breathing tube that had been inserted into her windpipe moments before. Later, he would convince the doctors to replace the trach ties with cotton straps, complaining that they, too, were too tight. Eventually, a nurse came over and loosened the tape. Katya's hand returned to its normal pinkish hue.

"She probably had an itty-bitty hand," I told him recently. He nodded. "It was an itty-bitty hand."

When Katya was five, we moved to Toronto, Canada, and her treatment continued at SickKids, the Hospital for Sick Children. There, the hospital staff awarded her a "Bravery Bead" for every blood withdrawal or surgery. Each of the beads corresponded to a different treatment. By the time it was over, Katya had upgraded from a bracelet to a necklace, which jangled with multicoloured beads that I would stare at, uncomprehending.

∞

My mother told me that the parents of healthy children simply "don't know the fear." Katya would often yank out her own trach tube in curiosity. At only five, I knew to flag down my father, who would dash over to re-insert the trach so she would not suffocate. "They don't know the worry," my mother says.

My parents became strict on roughhousing. Once, Katya and I were playing tag, and I accidentally knocked her down. Her lip, where most of the hemangioma was concentrated, started to bleed, and when her lip started to bleed, it was very difficult to stop.

My mother's face contorted with anger. She pointed a finger at me, telling me I knew better than to roughhouse with Katya. I watched as my parents descended on her, blocking her from my view. I began to see her as vulnerable, in need of our protection.

I had a combative spirit, my family tells me, even as early as the third grade. I would lash out at anyone who stared at Katya for a beat too long. When they looked in our general direction, I would stand in front of her like a 10-year-old wall, arms folded, until they were sufficiently intimidated and turned away.

Occasionally, my father will get a wistful look in his eyes and ask Katya whether she remembers having the trach. She doesn't remember much. But she remembers the balloon.

Once the hemangioma had receded, the trach was removed, which revealed deep scarring from five years of constant rubbing against the fragile hemangioma tissue. To mask the scar, doctors suggested a skin graft, which they accomplished by implanting a balloon into her chest and expanding it slowly over a period of a few months in order to stretch the skin, which would then be grafted onto the neck. The implant prevented her from getting involved in sports but she hadn't started playing seriously yet, so it didn't bother her. After the graft, she had to wear a neck brace to protect the delicate stitches.

"It was annoying," Katya says. "I felt like a dog in a cone. It was hard to get shirts on."

At school, her classmates would ask about the scar around her neck. She had only a limited understanding of her own medical situation, so she would shrug. They didn't know and neither did she. The confusion was mutual.

In seventh grade, an older boy took to calling her "Scarface." Katya pitied him; she told him the joke had little comedic value and that he ought to come up with something better.

She moved on to high school. There, she rose to popularity as one of the two point guards on the girls' basketball team. I went to a different school, an arts high school downtown. I was distraught by the thought of Katya navigating the treacherous waters of secondary school without me by her side, but from a distance, she seemed to be doing okay.

"Did someone cut your head off?" a boy once asked her.

"Oh my God, how did you *know*?" she responded. "Yeah, someone beheaded me and the doctors sewed my head back on. Don't tell anyone though." Later, when Katya saw him in the hallway, she mimed cutting off her head. His eyes widened in fear, and he never asked again.

∞

At 23, I learned that all of this could have been prevented. That is, if Katya had been diagnosed several years later.

The day I spoke with Dr. Portela, he mentioned that tracheotomies were now rarely performed on babies like Katya. My ears pricked up. I asked him how the approach had changed since then.

"There's a medicine called inderal, or propranolol," he told me. I had never heard of it. In 2008, he explained, nine years after my sister was diagnosed, a group of scientists made an accidental discovery. Propranolol, a beta-blocker normally used to treat conditions of the heart including chest pain and high blood pressure, could shrink infantile hemangioma.

It was shockingly effective. "Right now, your sister would have been treated with this medicine and wouldn't have needed a tracheotomy," he said.

He went on, "Nowadays, there are other types of tracheotomy tube holders or straps that keep the tube onto the neck that probably don't cause as much irritation to the neck skin." This, too, surprised me. But the tracheotomy itself would only be done now in the rare cases where the hemangioma was aggressive and unresponsive to treatment. "If you catch them early," he said, "you can prevent these secondary procedures."

I thought of all the "secondary procedures" Katya had undergone as a child. The surgeries, the teasing. Today, it would have all been avoided by a simple medication retailing for just 10 cents a tablet.

When the interview ended, I thanked Dr. Portela for his time, hung up the phone, and put my head in my hands. I had always thought of us as a family of the modern era. Yet here we were, constrained by the limitations of age, and by the cruel hand of time.

∞

When I told my parents about propranolol, my father was surprised but practical in his approach as always. "It came too late for her," he said simply. "But it's because of kids like Katya that they were able to find a treatment."

"If we had to wait for these advances, we wouldn't have her," my mother said.

I called Katya over video chat. She waved at me through the screen with a manicured hand. She was dressed in her usual athleisure get-up: hoodie, Adidas sweatpants and expensive running shoes.

When I told her about propranolol, she was unmoved. "Sometimes medicine misses you, sometimes it catches you."

It seemed I was the only one bothered by this wonderdrug. Again, I felt like an outsider, trying to make sense of a complex experience from the outside looking in. Katya added that her life as a patient had even informed her studies in nursing. "I know what it's like on the other side," she said. I shrugged, still miserable.

"Maybe it's part of the grieving process," Katya offered. "You're grieving a life that the person could have had."

I considered this. Was I still worried that she was vulnerable? That she had not lived a full life, despite our combined efforts? I realize, now, how wrong I truly was.

Marisa Coulton *is a journalist from Toronto, Ontario, who covers social justice, immigration, race and politics. Prior to attending Columbia Journalism School, she was Editor-in-Chief of Canada's oldest undergraduate history journal, The Mirror. She has also had her creative and academic work featured in the Canadian Journal of Undergraduate Research, and was published in the literary magazines Joyland, Untethered, Prairie Fire and Carousel. In her spare time, Marisa likes learning languages—she's currently working on Italian.*

Courtesy *@oldpicturebot.*

Death and Life in Wuhan

I'VE saved this picture in my phone for years. I have no clue where I first saw it. For a long time, it was a soothing presence for me — the quiet street, the bright paper cranes and the tinted green color presented an image of a city of peace and tranquility.

But lately, I have begun staring at it with horror. The only cyclist on the street is wearing a surgical mask. The street is eerily empty. I feel like I can hear sirens.

The picture was taken in April 2003, during the SARS outbreak. I was six years old then. I lived in Wuhan, which was far from the epicenter of the outbreak, but the fear still snuck up on me. Day after day I would sit in front of the television and watch news reports about the increasing death toll, my fingers fidgeting nervously.

The epidemic first emerged in November 2002 in Guangdong Province. In the beginning, the Chinese government downplayed the situation, but, by early April, with the increasing number of reported deaths, it started taking it very seriously. People began to panic as the central authorities called on the entire country to fight the virus.

One night, I turned my little wooden chair to face my dad and asked, "Are we all going to die?"

He laughed. "No, of course not. This is just happening in big cities, like Hong Kong or Beijing. Wuhan is not affected by it at all." My mother, however, frowned. She warned me to be careful with my words lest bad luck fall upon our family. But there was no more talk about SARS in my home. Still, my parents seemed to maintain a silent acknowledgment.

My dad's words comforted me, even as things began to change around me. There were rumors that vinegar fumes and Isatis root could ward off the disease. My parents panic-shopped. Goods all over the city were snapped up. The city smelled of vinegar. Every morning my parents had me drink herbal medicine from a plastic bag and the teachers at the kindergarten would check my temperature twice a day.

I repeated this ritual for two weeks, before being sent to my grandparents' home in the countryside. My dad told my uncle to keep the car window shut during the trip, as he worried that the pathogen might be in the air. "Back then, SARS didn't feel like something that was going to catch Wuhanese," my father now says. "But we still spent our time in anxiety, in gossip and in touch with online news."

I, however, enjoyed the five months I spent in the countryside. At dawn, my younger cousin and I would sneak into the vegetable farm next door to steal carrots. At night, we would catch fireflies. We helped deliver a baby goat. Looking back I now see that I invented my own fantasies about Wuhan's safety. I believed Wuhan, an inland city in China with no international fame, would always be too inconspicuous for God to spill disaster on it.

But now, 17 years later, everything has changed. Wuhan was picked this time. The global coronavirus pandemic began in Wuhan. And with that, my family and I became the story.

∞

On December 31, 2019, I spent a hopeful New Year's Eve in Times Square. The following morning I woke up to 12 notifications on my phone, including five from Weibo, the Chinese version of Twitter. I winced when I saw the words "SARS" and "Wuhan."

There were whispers that several people had been infected with a SARS-like disease in Wuhan, followed by a clarification by Wuhan Municipal Health Commission saying that this was a rumor. I called my parents to ask about the real situation.

My dad assured me that it couldn't be SARS. "No worries," he said in his usual casual and playful tone. "Our daily route is simple, we just travel between home and the office." I repeatedly reminded them to wear masks when they were outside. He promised they would.

The panic and worry subsided but not for long. Two weeks later my dad shared an article from the US-Doctor WeChat subscription, which reported that two people were confirmed dead of the new coronavirus in Wuhan. He asked me to reconsider my plan to return home during the March spring break.

He called again several hours later to tell me that my grandfather, who had advanced lung cancer, had been encouraged to leave the hospital in Wuhan, as a patient on the same floor was suspected of having coronavirus. The city's healthcare system was strained and my grandfather said his bed was needed. Meanwhile, my aunts and cousins had all flown to Wuhan to celebrate the Chinese New Year with my dying grandfather.

I was struggling to grasp the situation in which my family found itself. "Wait, so you know how serious the situation is and you guys still decided to gather together in Wuhan? At this moment?" I was furious.

I sent my father a BBC story, which reported that "the number of people already infected by the mystery virus emerging in China is far greater than official figures suggest." U.K. experts estimated the figure to be nearer 1,700.

He laughed. "I don't trust these numbers," he said. "The Chinese media is transparent now, otherwise people would denounce it." He then jumped to another topic, asking me to say hi to all my relatives.

I began to count. One, two, three…There were now eight people in my house. I tried to calm myself. But I failed. I was desperate.

Two days later, the government confirmed that there was evidence of the spread of the coronavirus in the community and that people were infecting each other. I stayed up all night, panic-buying food, alcohol spray and masks online to be delivered to my parents. But no deliveries were being made during a festival week. And some companies were refusing to make deliveries to Hubei Province. I bombarded my parents with hundreds of messages that night, completely ignoring their replies that I go to sleep.

Though my relatives were silent about the virus in our family WeChat group, I could sense the anxiety in my father's voice when we spoke on the phone. They had all left Wuhan for their own homes, he told me. Meanwhile, my grandfather decided to go back to Yichang, his hometown, knowing he had not much time left.

A week had passed and now without warning, Wuhan ordered a shutdown as the government tried to halt the spread of the virus. Many people were still asleep when the order was issued, including my parents, who intended to go back to Yichang to take care of my grandfather that day.

As a child, I had seen the SARS epidemic as a summer fantasy. Now I persuaded myself that the quarantine could be an extended holiday for my family. My father could quit smoking and take on more house cleaning. My mother could use the time to take online English classes. We made a family plan to read the same book every week and share our written reviews about it each Sunday.

Like the government of Wuhan, I tried to put a gentle face on this deadly disease. But when I got a video call from my mother late at night on February 27, I realized that my efforts to see the good side were at best naïve.

"I don't have my father anymore," she said, her voice thick and choked. Her eyes were red-rimmed. My grandfather had died, far from his children. His body was placed in a white body bag and transported to a funeral home in Yichang. My grandmother was not allowed to follow the hearse.

My grandfather had been a proper soldier all his life. He was always fastidious. He would not go out until he had combed his hair carefully and made sure that his clothes and shoes matched. He hoped that when he left us, his intimate personal things could be properly placed in a wooden box. His children and grandchildren would gather around it to accompany my grandmother.

But everything happened so quickly and there was no time to linger over details. The instructions he had left for his funeral could not be met.

My grandmother sighed, saying that the clothes left by my neat and careful grandfather gave her the feeling that her husband still lived. When she went through his closet, she could still smell him. But the virus continued its destructive path and his clothes had to be burned, isolating my grandmother even more.

"I imagined my father dying, but I never thought that I could not be with him," my mother said. "I should have left Wuhan earlier."

∞

The lockdown of Wuhan ended after three months on April 8. My father returned to work and my mother immediately drove back to Yichang to see her father's grave. Wuhan's emergence from quarantine came as the city where I had come for graduate school, New York, was becoming a world epicenter of the virus, with hundreds of people dying every day.

Like in that photograph I carried with me, people in New York were wearing face masks and the streets were eerily quiet.

If there is an equivalent to the paper cranes, perhaps it is the sound I hear across the city every night at 7 p.m. when people open their windows to bang on pots and pans and clap their hands as thanks to all the healthcare workers. I don't need to imagine the sound of ambulances. I can hear them all day and night.

When the lockdown of Wuhan came to an end on April 8, I wrote my grandfather this short letter:

I hope the tea is good and strong and the food fresh and that the weather is still sunny enough to sit outside on one of those wooden benches. I hope people there will love your fancy clothes as well as your bad jokes and poker face. It's funny how people say better days are ahead. They are.

Jingyi He *is a journalist from Wuhan, China, who covers human interest stories with beats including culture, entertainment and religion. She has traveled across three continents for various journalism internships, during which she produced written features and video pieces. Upon graduating from Columbia Journalism School, Jingyi plans to work as a reporter or anchor for a newsroom. When she's not working, she's usually traveling, watching an unhealthy amount of television or chatting with friends.*

AUTHORS

Anaïs Amin

Kyra Aurelia Alessandrini

Allison Arnold

Marisa Elena Nicole Coulton

Claire Fox

Grace Elizabeth Goodwin

Jingyi He

Circe Hughes

AUTHORS

Serena McNiff

Benoit Morenne

Thomas Christopher Nocera

Oheneba Ama Nti Osei

Rachel Jacqueline Pilgrim

Christy Marie Piña

Marissa Roberge

Hayley Vaughn

Made in the USA
Columbia, SC
20 May 2020

97561668R00079